A heartfelt dialogue where deep friendship becomes the channel for timeless Buddhist insight. – **Dame Christiana Figueres**, Former Head of UN Climate Change Convention

This thoroughly enjoyable book offers a delightful mixture of straightforward yet profound Buddhist teaching, woven through the inspiring journey of a pioneering Buddhist nun. Reflections on transformative spiritual wisdom and a courageous engagement with the intersecting issues of patriarchy and climate change are offered in a way that is accessible to beginners, and rewarding for those steeped in these themes. – **Yanai Postelnik**, senior Insight Meditation teacher and climate activist

What Are You Waiting For? is my top recommendation for newcomers to Buddhism. With clear explanations of core Buddhist principles and a concise account of the movement for full ordination for women – woven through Santacitta Bhikkhuni's striking and relatable personal journey – this book is engaging, informative, and inspiring. – **Santussika Bhikkhuni**, founder of Karuna Buddhist Vihara

It is always heartening to hear of the Buddhist path discussed through the deep relationship of a long friendship. Venerable Santacitta and Irmgard offer us a living example of *kalyana mitra*, beneficial spiritual friendship. – **Maura Sills**, founder of the Karuna Institute and Honorary Fellow of the UK Council for Psychotherapy

In this book, my dear friend Santacitta Bhikkhuni shares a tender, fearless account of her Dharma journey. With clarity and compassion, and the rare perspective of a bhikkhuni, she brings ancient wisdom into the challenges of our time. A moving, honest offering for anyone seeking depth, meaning, and liberation. – **Thanissara**, Dharma teacher and author of *Time to Stand Up: An Engaged Buddhist Manifesto for Our Earth*

The brilliance of this spiritual conversation is in the relationship of the authors, in how they describe the relational nature of the teachings, and in how it is possible to contribute to reconditioning the unconsciousness of supremacy as a spiritual practice and endeavour, be it for patriarchy or other oppressions. The title of the book indicates such a beautifully posed question because the recorded dialogue provides such wide-open doors for all of us to journey into and explore, for our collective awakening and greater freedom. – **Larry Yang**, author of *Awakening Together: The Spiritual Practice of Inclusivity and Community*

WHAT ARE YOU WAITING FOR?

A Conversation about Buddhism between Two Old Friends

Irmgard Kirchner &
Santacitta Bhikkhuni

Translated from the German
by Gwen Clayton

Windhorse Publications
38 Newmarket Road
Cambridge CB5 8DT
info@windhorsepublications.com
windhorsepublications.com

© Irmgard Kirchner and Santacitta Bhikkhuni, 2026
© English translation, Gwen Clayton, 2026

The right of Irmgard Kirchner and Santacitta Bhikkhuni to be identified as the authors of this work has been asserted by them in accordance with the Copyright, Designs and Patents Act 1988.

No portion of this book may be utilized in any form for the training, development, enhancement, or operation of any artificial intelligence technologies. This prohibition includes all forms of AI, including generative models, neural networks, and any other types of computational intelligence. This restriction extends to all methods of obtaining or utilizing data, including but not limited to data scraping, data mining, direct or indirect observation, manual entry, or any innovative data-sourcing techniques that might be developed in the future.

Cover design: Priyada
Cover image: Emanuel Aeneas Megersa
Illustrations: Nikkolo Feuermacher
Typesetting: Tarajyoti

British Library Cataloguing in Publication Data:
A catalogue record for this book is available from the British Library.

ISBN 978-1-915342-55-3

Praise for *What Are You Waiting For? A Conversation about Buddhism between Two Old Friends*

In this book, Ayya Santacitta imparts decades of accumulated spiritual wisdom to inspire and orient us to a better way of living. Ayya shares her fascinating story while elucidating deep Buddhist concepts in an engaging, down-to-earth, conversational style with her lifelong journalist friend. Whether renouncing her bohemian life to become a Buddhist nun, leaving her patriarchal community to be a female pioneer in the Buddhist world, or her straight talk about the climate crisis, Ayya's life is an uncompromising, courageous expression of living in truth. By her example, she invites the reader to use teachings to likewise find courage and fearlessness to discover peace within while making this a better world. A real gem of a book! – **James Baraz**, co-author of *Awakening Joy: 10 Steps to Happiness*, co-founding teacher Spirit Rock Meditation Center

Ayya Santacitta has given us a Dharma book of great breadth and depth. Her book offers us the fresh experience of hearing the thinking processes of a nun who has devoted her life to Buddhist practice. Through conversations with an old friend, she speaks with a voice that is authoritative from her many years of study and practice as a nun, yet also intimate with personal details. The book covers a wide range of subjects, from basic Buddhist teachings on the four foundations of mindfulness, the seven factors of awakening, and the Four Noble Truths, all the way to more esoteric subjects such as rebirth and merit-making, and current events regarding ordination of bhikkhunis and the climate crisis. Relevant both for beginning practitioners and those with lots of experience, engrossing and engaging, this book is a pleasure to read! – **Rebecca Bradshaw**, author of *Down to Earth Dharma: Insight Meditation to Awaken the Heart* and Guiding Teacher Emeritus of the Insight Meditation Society

This intimate and refreshingly honest dialogue between two lifelong friends offers a rare window into the living heart of contemporary Buddhism. With warmth, courage, and deep insight, Santacitta Bhikkhuni shares her remarkable journey — one that bridges East and West, tradition and innovation, contemplation and activism. This book speaks to anyone seeking a path of meaning and liberation amidst the complexity of modern life. A wise and inspiring companion for those drawn to the Dharma, especially in these urgent and tender times. – **Mark Coleman**, Dharma teacher, author, founder of Awake in the Wild

Weaving together Santacitta Bhikkhuni's fascinating life story with easy-to-read descriptions of the basics of Buddhism, this book reveals her adventurous spirit, fearless moral courage, and deep spiritual commitment. From embarking on a round-the-world trip on the spur of the moment, to being one of the first women to ordain as a Theravada nun in the US, to creating a unique temple-space integrating Dhamma, ecology, and art, Santacitta Bhikkhuni has consistently challenged outdated social and religious norms. – **Kate Davies D.Phil.**, Board Chair and President of the Saranaloka Foundation, author of *Intrinsic Hope: Living Courageously in Troubled Times*

Ayya Santacitta's new book is a delight. She presents her biography in the form of a dialogue with an old friend. In the process, she spotlights the key moments that illuminate her personal spiritual journey and answers foundational Dharma questions for the readers. We see how her life traverses tradition and innovation, leaving a legacy for others to follow. Her genuine Dharma commitment and wisdom shine through on every page. – **Khenmo Konchog Drolma**, Abbess of Vajra Dakini Nunnery

Contents

Foreword by Jetsunma Tenzin Palmo   ix
Dedication and Authors' Acknowledgements   xi
Publisher's Acknowledgements   xii

Introduction   1
Wide Open Doors   5
Finding the Middle Way   29
Healing and Moving Forward   41
Practising Emptiness   61
A Dent in the Patriarchy   75
The Power to Say No   93
Emotions and Mindfulness   111
Buddhism in Daily Life   119
What Are You Waiting For? Buddhism Here and Now   133
The Next Steps on the Path: Santacitta Bhikkhuni Explains the Aloka Earth Room Concept   141

Appendix 1:   Biography of Santacitta Bhikkhuni   147
Appendix 2:   Short Biography of Irmgard Kirchner   153
Appendix 3:   Short Biography of Gwen Clayton   155

Contents

Appendix 4: Bhikkhuni Ordination in the Theravada Tradition of Buddhism: A Conversation between Irmgard Kirchner and Ute Hüsken, Professor of South Asian Cultural and Religious History at the University of Heidelberg   157

Appendix 5: Thirty-Seven Qualities That Inspire Awakening (*bodhipakkhiya-dhamma*)   165

Notes   169

Foreword

Although nowadays Buddhism has become increasingly popular and well known in the West, still there is a need for books that explain the basic Dharma principles in a manner both interesting and informative. Many Buddhist books are too technical and complex for a beginner, and there is a need for something more approachable and also relevant to our contemporary times.

Since this book is set out as a dialogue between two old friends, it deals with many topics that a standard book on Buddhism would not cover. When a book is interesting and helpful, we read and absorb with enthusiasm and can grasp the information effortlessly.

Ven. Santacitta has spent many years in formal meditation practice and has also been teaching Buddhism in the West, where she understands the difficulties that are faced in our present society. Since she trained as a nun within a male monastic environment, she herself has dealt with many challenges throughout the years.

Buddhism is a science of the mind aimed at understanding how we experience our reality through a distorted lens that causes our problems and discontent. We are shown how to transform our consciousness and bring about genuine happiness that is not reliant on mere outer pleasant circumstances. The key is our state of mind. Step by step, the path leads towards greater peace and understanding, more kindness and compassion, and the deep inner joy of freedom. We ourselves must walk the path. But here is a good guide for the journey!

Jetsunma Tenzin Palmo
Dongyu Gatsal Ling
January 2025

Dedication and Authors' Acknowledgements

For Maria and Karl, Helga and Josef,
our parents in this life.

Thanks to Klaus Kirchner.

Thanks to the Bess Family Foundation, who sponsored the English translation of the German original.

Thanks to Gwen Clayton for translating this book into English and to the Windhorse Publications team for the many tasks involved in publishing the English translation.

Thanks to Emanuel Aeneas Megersa, Friederike Bayer, Sepp Bayer, Jennifer Byrne, Nikkolo Feuermacher, Ute Hüsken, Gerhard Jäger, Franziska Kasper, Louije Kim, Maria Kirchner, Thomas Kussin, Eva Maria Ocherbauer, Doris Pust, Ursula Richard, Stephanie Schmiederer.

Publisher's Acknowledgements

We would like to thank the individuals who supported this book through our 'Sponsor-a-book' campaign (www.windhorsepublications.com/sponsor) and the Friends of Windhorse Publications initiative (www.windhorsepublications.com/friends).

Windhorse Publications wish to gratefully acknowledge a grant from Future Dharma and the Triratna European Chairs' Assembly Fund towards the production of this book.

FUTURE DHARMA

Introduction

This book grew out of several long conversations and a friendship that spans over forty years. I first met my friend Sylvia in Vienna when I was nineteen. Today she goes by the name Santacitta Bhikkhuni. If one addresses her formally, her name takes the prefix 'Venerable'.[1] The flamboyant cultural anthropology student and dance theatre performer whom I once knew has become an internationally active and renowned nun, teacher, and monastery founder. Meanwhile, I have become a journalist whose work is motivated and nourished by encounters and conversations with other people.

We have stayed in touch as friends over the years, even when our lives began to take very different paths. We have exchanged news regularly, meeting up or talking to each other by phone or online, and have always enjoyed bringing together worldly and spiritual perspectives on things. Work, relationships, male dominance, separation and new beginnings, difficulties and successes exist in the monastic life just as in the worldly one, even if they are assessed differently.

Through her international teaching activity, Santacitta Bhikkhuni is involved with the climate movement, with women's issues, and with diversity. These are areas that are important to both of us, the nun and the journalist. Here, too, worldly and the spiritual views can coincide with or supplement each other, and our dialogue has become well established over the course of many years.

Having said that, these years have also seen a distinct shift in the questions I have asked Santacitta Bhikkhuni: while I initially followed her life with wonder tinged with a certain scepticism, because of her choices and achievements as well as my own experiences with meditation, my interest in Buddhism has gradually grown. When she stayed in Austria for a few months recently I finally had the opportunity to ask her all the questions that interested me so much. I would never have been able to ask these questions of another Buddhist teacher, either as a private individual or as a journalist, and I think Santacitta Bhikkhuni would not have answered these questions in the same way if they had been posed by anyone else.

Following an intense monastic training, Santacitta Bhikkhuni left the lineage with which she had trained, a traditional and internationally well-known lineage of the Thai Forest Tradition of Buddhism. In this lineage, women are still denied the possibility of full ordination as bhikkhunis or nuns. In California, Santacitta Bhikkhuni co-founded a new Buddhist monastery for women. This step was significant not just for her as a person, but also for the position of women in the Buddhist world.

The conversations with Santacitta Bhikkhuni are followed by an interview with Ute Hüsken, Professor of Cultural and Religious History of South Asia at the University of Heidelberg. This short text serves to explain the modern bhikkhuni ordination and can also be read as an introduction to this book.

Introduction

The conversations that gave rise to this book took place in German in autumn 2021, in Vienna and in a small village in Hungary. In them, Santacitta Bhikkhuni, who lives in the United States and is globally active, answers questions posed by me, a journalist based in Central Europe whose thoughts and attitudes are inevitably shaped by the sociopolitical discourse emerging there. The intense discussions took place over a short period, so that each conversation picked up where the previous one had ended. There is therefore a thread running through this book, which may not be immediately discernible if the chapters are read separately. Sometimes an answer does not appear to respond directly to the question being asked. Some topics come up repeatedly and are discussed differently depending on the context. Individual questions remain unanswered because they are impossible to answer from a Buddhist perspective. The result of these discussions is a unique fabric of thoughts, personal experiences, and Buddhist teachings. For me, it has shed light on what living Buddhism means and what it can achieve.

The final chapter, 'The Next Steps on the Path', was written for the English translation in the United States in autumn 2024.

Irmgard Kirchner

Wide Open Doors

You have been a Buddhist for more than thirty years. How did you get into Buddhism? How do you see your path to Buddhism, looking back on it today?

I lived in Vienna in the 1980s – you and I already knew each other then – and, looking back, I was pretty directionless. I was working at the Serapionstheater[2] and studying cultural and social anthropology, two callings that meant a great deal to me. But, although my life was very interesting, there was something profoundly lacking that I did not truly understand. At that time, I regularly smoked hashish, and my romantic relationships were not really fulfilling.

I was searching for something, for a direction that would give my life stability. It did not need to be simple, but it had to be meaningful, whatever it might be. Something that would lead to a deeper wisdom and harmony with things as they really are. But I would not have been able to express it in these words at the time.

As a teenager I travelled to Africa with my parents a few times. There I saw how the Maasai lived. I had the impression that the Maasai were more in touch with reality than people from my own culture. In their unique way of being, they seemed to me much less affected than the people I had known up to then. This fascinated me, and I hoped that cultural and social anthropology, the subject that I later studied at university, would be able to teach me this knowledge.

However, it soon became clear to me that this was a subject that was, at the time, concerned above all with observing people from other cultures and how they managed their lives, and then comparing and evaluating them. It did not offer me any real answers, and my original interest began to wane.

Did you begin your search early on?
Yes. As a child I went with my brother to a summer camp in former Yugoslavia several times. There were children from many countries there, children who did not speak German. It was clear to me already then that I would need to go somewhere else one day, somewhere where they did not speak my mother tongue, and that I would live in many different places far from my homeland and study something. But of course, I had no idea what it would be.

So you looked for a wisdom teaching that would suit you?
Yes, some system or other, it did not matter what. I only knew that Christianity, the only spiritual teaching that I had had any experience with, did not speak to me, although I had happy memories of my time at a kindergarten run by nuns. As a child growing up, I also went into the church behind our house from time to time. I liked the rituals, and one could meet boys there. I was fascinated by the statues of the saints with their long, flowing, golden robes. I wanted to meet people like that in real life. I never thought of myself as religious in the traditional sense, but the representations of people who were 'realized' made a deep impression on me already then.

What does 'realized' mean, and did you already have a mental image of it then?
'Realized' means something like 'healed' – healed of ignorance, healed from delusions. 'Holy' and 'healed' have the same linguistic root. Already then, I was convinced that such people actually existed, and that there were systems that could bring about this healing process, that could make someone holy. I just didn't know where one could find such people.

My next clue came from the Maasai: the instinctive impression I got was that there was something in their knowledge and lifestyle that my own culture had lost. For the longest time I had the romantic notion that people who lived simply and apart from Western consumerism were automatically wise. However, after spending a year living with a Muslim fishing family on a small island in South Thailand in 1988, I came to realize that living simply and remotely on its own does not necessarily lead to wisdom.

I remember that you wanted to do some fieldwork for your cultural and social anthropology studies there.
I had a mixture of motivations. I romanticized the situation – the way cultural anthropologists often do when they start out – and wanted to immerse myself in this, from my standpoint, very different culture and 'become one of them'. And then I was also in love with a young man, the oldest son of the fishing family that I lived with. He later died of drug abuse.

Did you think the people you romanticized were closer to the truth, too?
Yes, I did. But then I discovered that the man I loved was addicted to drugs and this shattered my fantasies to a certain

extent. I now see what a destructive effect tourism had on the island. It disrupted traditional life and drew young people away from the stability of their families and elders.

I grew up in a relatively affluent family and was able to do many of the things that I wanted. Looking back now, I think I probably received too little guidance from my parents. Other than my initial training, people seldom told me what to do. I attended a prestigious private hotel-management school. And then an even more expensive one, where I could take the secondary-school leaving exam. But it was never my intention to work in my parents' hotel; I always felt drawn to study cultural and social anthropology.

Did you already know that then?
Yes. I wanted to connect with a wisdom teaching. I was deeply drawn to this type of idea, and also had a formative experience around this time. I was hiking with a friend in the Salzkammergut region of Austria. Deep in the forest we came across a large mansion in the middle of a clearing. The doors were open, and we went inside. The house must have been the headquarters of a masonic lodge. In a huge hall there was a long table with chairs, just like a knights' table in a film. There were curious objects displayed on the walls and ceiling that seemed magical to me. In any event it was a fascinating place. Then we heard someone coming and slipped out again.

But I was reminded of this calling: the fact that there were these belief systems and that I wanted to connect to one of them. I did not want to force anything, but rather nourish the calling and see where it would take me. When my mother died in a riding accident in 1986, I felt a deep sense of urgency. Her death made me very aware of a trait shared by my female relatives. The women of my ancestral line, both on my father's and on my mother's side, all had one thing in common: as companions to strong men, they had never really developed their own potential. My mother was very beautiful and had always seemed content to me while she was young. With the start of the menopause, as her beauty began to change, she became depressed. She died at the age of 48, shortly after her own mother's death.

I was then twenty-eight and became the oldest woman in my immediate family. The psychological strain that I inherited at this time seemed ominous, and I was frightened by it. My mother took sleeping pills and antidepressants – something that I definitely didn't want to do. I knew with certainty that there were other ways of dealing with such challenges, even if they were not necessarily easy.

My mother left me some money. In 1987 a friend of mine set off on a round-the-world trip. I happened to have some time between two theatre productions, and decided on the spur of the moment to accompany her for the first three months. Four days later I was in Bangkok. I still did not know what I was looking for, but I had the feeling that I was getting closer. I had no inkling at the time that it would be a religion. I saw Buddhist temples and Buddhist monks and nuns. Interesting, I thought – but that was it.

Then we continued on to Myanmar. Thirty years ago one met few travellers from the West there. There were no Western consumer goods, and our stay was limited to one week. It was just like going back in time. On a train journey from Mandalay to the capital, Rangoon, I saw two Buddhist monks on a station platform. All of the people around them prostrated themselves and threw themselves onto the dirty floor. Those must be very highly respected monks, I thought, at once fascinated and appalled. Then both of the monks sat down near us in our carriage. It was May, and very hot and stuffy. The train was teeming with people; they were even on the roof. It was an unbelievable chaos. The two monks were holding fans and sat there for hours, quiet and calm, in contrast to all the other travellers.

I looked over at them again and again, asking myself: what do they know, that they can be so still, surrounded by all this turmoil? For everyone else, me included, the heat was simply unbearable. The monks' equanimity made a very deep impression on me.

Then we travelled back to South Thailand. There we met the young fisherman whom I fell in love with. A year later I returned to Thailand again, to start a field research project surrounded by his family.

When and how did you really come into contact with Buddhism?
While I was staying with my boyfriend's family, I went to another island to run some errands. There in South Thailand, about four hours' drive from the border with Malaysia, I saw a young Western man at the bus station, dressed all in white and with a shaved head. I was curious and spoke to him. It turned out that he was Austrian and had attended the same hotel-management school in Salzburg as me, two years earlier. When I asked him what he was doing and why he looked like that, he explained to me that he lived in a nearby monastery.

Wat Suan Mokkh, the monastery of Ajahn Buddhadasa,[3] was only a couple of kilometres away. He recommended that I visit it one day.

At the time I did not know how famous Ajahn Buddhadasa was in Thailand. Nonetheless I gave back my ticket for the onward journey, got in a taxi and went to the monastery. I wanted to see it, and I told myself that I could of course leave at any time. Three days after my arrival in April 1988, one of the monthly meditation retreats began. These took place regularly in English, from the first to the tenth of every month. I was convinced that after three to four days I would be slipping out through the back door.

Everything was extremely simple and austere. I would not have thought that I would manage to spend ten days sleeping on a thin mat on a concrete floor and getting up at four every morning. We meditated according to a fixed schedule and received instructions in English. We washed ourselves at a giant basin by pouring water over our bodies with a small jug, the way people in rural Asia do. I liked this simple lifestyle very much. It felt as if I had done all of this once before.

Ajahn Buddhadasa reminded me of the monks I had seen on the train in Myanmar a year earlier. I thought, 'He knows how one becomes like those monks', and I stayed. During the first three weeks after I started to meditate, many strange images rose up from my subconscious. I only understood later that these were images from the Vajrayana tradition of Buddhism, images of rituals and dances in a cave.

Following my return from the monastery to the fishing village, I practised a lot of yoga and released these sensations emerging from my subconscious until the images disappeared. In these first three weeks a great many things surfaced in my mind. Sometimes the image of a Tibetan teacher flashed up. I thought that it would become clear eventually who my Tibetan teacher was. At this point I simply wanted to stay in Wat Suan Mokkh, close to Ajahn Buddhadasa. What was going on in my mind at that time was more than enough.

I listened to the teachings. My English was not particularly good then, and I did not yet speak any Thai. Nevertheless, I understood a little. There were lightbulb moments when I thought: there are words to describe what I vaguely sense! There is in fact a whole body of teachings about this, and it is called Buddhism! Suddenly many things fell into place, in my thinking and in my life. It was as if a part of my being that had been idle had suddenly been supplied with energy. I had very little doubt, as if I was already familiar with these teachings from some earlier time. The most convincing element for me was the presence of Ajahn Buddhadasa.

In the years that followed I returned to this monastery time and again and took part in many more such ten-day retreats. Later I also helped out there. From the time of my first retreat, I wanted to be near the monastery, but I did not want to live there – that only came later.

I remember that you also had some traumatic experiences during this period.

My boyfriend, the young Muslim fisherman, died as a result of drug abuse. In my arms! We had travelled to an Akha village in the mountains of North Thailand. The Akha belong to the traditional communities known as 'hill tribes' in Thailand. I wanted to get away from the island and from the big cities where he could buy himself drugs.

We had been in the village for about a week when my boyfriend died of an overdose of opium combined with his withdrawal medication. I remember driving down through the forest to the provincial capital of Chiang Mai that night in a jeep, accompanied by police and my boyfriend's body. Below in the city I had to wait in a guest house until my boyfriend's parents arrived from South Thailand to collect his body. And then in my confusion I stumbled into a motorbike in the street. It was really an impossible situation: my lower thigh was broken. My boyfriend's parents took me to a hospital and got hold of a relative who stayed with me. After the operation I wanted to return to Austria as soon as possible to check how successful the treatment had been – and, as became clear later, it was perfect.

When I came to arrange my return journey to Austria, I remembered a travel agency at the port, managed by an efficient man, a jack-of-all-trades, who would be able to sort everything out for me. This acquaintance would later become my husband, but at the time the idea could not have been further from my mind. I was in shock. Two years earlier my mother had died, then my boyfriend, and now the fiasco with the accident. In exchange for cash, the man took me, all my luggage, and my crutches to the aeroplane. When we said goodbye, I thanked him and said he could visit me whenever he was in Europe.

He turned up at my place in Austria quite soon afterwards. I very much wanted to go back to Thailand, but at the time I did not think I could manage it by myself. I did not want to enter the monastery, I did not want to become a nun, but

I wanted to be nearby. I had idealistic notions about how I could make use of my background in hotel management and cultural and social anthropology. Furthermore, in the early 1980s I was a co-founder of one of the first intentional community-living projects just outside Vienna.[4]

I wanted to establish an eco-resort on a piece of land belonging to my deceased boyfriend's family, and in so doing bring in fair employment opportunities for people who could not find work or performed the most menial tasks, such as the Chao Le or Moken, a nation in the south of Thailand and Myanmar, whose name literally means 'Sea People'. Most Sea People live a semi-nomadic hunter-gatherer lifestyle based on the sea, and travel from island to island in accordance with the seasons.

My Thai acquaintance was the manager of a travel agency and a restaurant. I thought that I could work with him, and so I got mixed up in this peculiar love story. At the time I did not know that he was a criminal. Following my return to Thailand in 1989 I worked as the local representative of an Austrian travel agency in various luxury hotels. My new boyfriend liked this: he was a bon vivant who constantly lived beyond his means, as I was to discover only later. It was an unhappy time for me. I suffered from depression and struggled with low energy. I knew I had to go to the monastery, but I was not yet ready. When I think back to that time today, I can see that I was experiencing some deep inner restructuring. I was becoming increasingly aware of my real priorities, and I knew that I had to organize my life around them.

Looking back, I can say that I did have good ideas but that I lacked the maturity required to put them into practice. I even married my friend and hoped-for business partner, in part to get easier access to a long-stay visa for Thailand. However, he turned out to be a member of the Thai tourist mafia. I was simply much too inexperienced at the time and had no idea about crime. After the wedding it dawned on me that there might be something wrong with my Thai husband.

Happily, I was financially independent from him. I withdrew into Ajahn Buddhadasa's monastery again and again. My husband would come to collect me and beg me to return, promising to change, but this never happened.

This sounds quite crazy: how did you put up with all this as an educated and independent woman?

As complicated and chaotic as my private life was, life in the monastery was very simple. I did not want to take part in one retreat after another. I wanted to have my own house in Wat Suan Mokkh and live there. A Brazilian woman whom I had got to know in the monastery once took me along to another Buddhist monastery. Straight away the abbot there gave me my own kuti, a small house for meditation and sleeping, and promised to instruct me. I wanted to stay with Ajahn Buddhadasa, since I felt a very strong connection to him, but the offer gave me courage. At that time, Ajahn Buddhadasa was no longer abbot of Wat Suan Mokkh since he had become too old. But I went to the new abbot, Ajahn Bo, and told him about the other monastery and the kuti that I had been offered and stressed that I would prefer to stay near Ajahn Buddhadasa, but that I would only stay if I could have a kuti here, too. I asked for a specific kuti, next to that of a former female university professor who was the second most important teacher at the monastery after Ajahn Buddhadasa. Within a couple of hours, I was given the key to the kuti I had wished for. It was a large, beautiful old wooden house with an upper floor for meditation.

I wanted to show my appreciation for the generosity that the monastery had shown me, so I went to the kitchen and asked whether I could help out there. I started going there at 4 am every day and working there for two to three hours. Ajahn Buddhadasa could see that I was doing well, since the women in the kitchen saw me every day. I no longer took part in the retreats very often. It was clear to me that I had a difficult process ahead of me, which I had to work through myself. Ajahn Buddhadasa gave me a great deal of spiritual support.

Every day he would come out of his kuti and sit on the bench outside for a couple of hours. I often sat down nearby, simply to spend time in his presence. Very early every morning, when it was still cool, he would walk a hundred paces, supported by two young monks. That was his morning exercise. At this time, he was already eighty-three and could only walk with difficulty.

I wanted to establish a relationship with him, although it was not really possible to talk to him. It was evident to me that it had to be a wordless kind of contact. On his daily walk he always passed a tree under which a nun laid a white cloth at night to catch the fallen blossoms. She made medicine from them. I knew that Ajahn Buddhadasa went past the tree every day and offered to help the nun collect the blossoms. Every time that Ajahn Buddhadasa went past, he stopped, turned to me, and looked into my eyes for a couple of seconds. That was our daily ritual. Do you know the expression 'darshan'? People who are realized can pass on energy, by looking into your eyes, through touch, or through a piece of food that they have blessed. It was just such a transfer of energy that took place here. Every day, I do not know how many times. At the beginning I was full of doubt about whether I should divorce my husband. I told my story to the experienced teacher who lived next door to me. She practically commanded me to do so: you need to get divorced straight away!

With the unexpected help of people whom I hardly knew, I then got divorced very quickly and with few complications, although my marriage had taken place in Austria. Everyone involved knew that I was a student of Ajahn Buddhadasa and that I had had no idea of my spouse's criminal background. The fact that I was with Ajahn Buddhadasa seems to have been significant, and in retrospect I think this is why everyone helped me. Once I had decided that I wanted to get divorced, everything came together and within a few hours the matter was accomplished. It was quite remarkable.

Up until that time I had tried to struggle along in various different directions, but it had not worked. All the doors in my life had closed except one, which stood wide open: the door into the monastery. Then I knew that I was on the right path. After the divorce I moved into the monastery completely and spent another year living there before returning to Europe. Ajahn Buddhadasa got steadily weaker, and it was clear that he would soon die. I knew that when this happened, I would no longer want to be there.

Did you already want to be a nun at that time? What was your role in the monastery?

I was a lay sister, an upasika. I dressed very simply in a black or brown sarong[5] with a white or brown blouse. I was certain about one thing – I did not want to be ordained as a Western nun in Asia. I did not want to have a special status. As a farang, a Westerner, I would somehow always have remained at the edge of the community. The system in the monastery was also too patriarchal for me. I wanted to go back to the West, but at the time I was not sure where I should go.

The forest monastery of Suan Mokkh was very beautiful and had been designed in a very unusual way by Ajahn Buddhadasa. In contrast to other monasteries in Thailand, there were no golden temple complexes, and there was only a single Buddha statue in the whole monastery. Ajahn Buddhadasa had attempted to free Buddhism from superstition and from those ideas that Westerners liked to look down on. He wanted to demonstrate that Buddhism was an art and a science. This reflected the zeitgeist in Thailand at the time, and he was one of the pioneers of this trend. Intellectuals from Bangkok flocked to him. He was an important reformer of Buddhism, although I did not know this at the time. I had ended up in Wat Suan Mokkh purely by chance.

Initially all this seemed normal to me. This is just how it is in a monastery, I thought, and it was just the right monastery for me. Ajahn Buddhadasa had had eccentric buildings constructed: two huge ships made of concrete. Inside one of them was the library, with a big Dharma hall above it. The second ship was used to collect water during the rainy season. There was also an art gallery, the 'Spiritual Theatre'. The artworks were used to teach the principles of the Dharma,[6] which is the Sanskrit word for the Buddha's teachings. What Ajahn Buddhadasa did at the time was actually very innovative.

At Wat Suan Mokkh all the schools of Buddhism were present. There was literature and art from the Theravada, Mahayana, and Vajrayana schools. The first book that I was given to read there was *Zen Mind, Beginner's Mind* by Shunryū Suzuki.[7] This was Ajahn Buddhadasa's recommendation for beginners. He himself had translated two works of the Zen tradition from English into Thai. The approach of the Thai Forest Tradition is similar to that of other Buddhist traditions such as Japanese Zen, Chinese Chan, and Tibetan Dzogchen and Mahamudra.

Naturally there were some who criticized Ajahn Buddhadasa. He was accused of not teaching true Buddhism, but with his powerful intellect he was always able to defend his position. Highly intelligent and realized as he was, he could afford criticism and continued to gather more and more people from different countries around him. His style was confrontational, in part because he was so ahead of his time. He is considered a pioneer of what is today known as Engaged Buddhism. He was already speaking about environmental protection and climate change in the 1980s.

Did you ever speak to him personally, or have a consultation with him?
No. Naturally I listened to his instruction. But we had contact without speaking to each other. I just knew that I was not supposed to talk to him. Because we never spoke to each other,

our intuitive connection became ever stronger, in the same way that, for a blind person, the other senses become sharper. I just relied completely on my intuition. Ajahn Buddhadasa gave me very strong spiritual support, the certainty that I did not need to be afraid, whatever happened. I did not need any more than that from him.

Around the time when it became clear that he would soon die, and when I realized I did not want to stay in Wat Suan Mokkh any longer, I found, in our small meditation hall for Westerners, a chanting book – a sort of songbook or prayer book – from Amaravati monastery[8] in the United Kingdom. Immediately I thought, that is where I will go next. In September 1992 I left Wat Suan Mokkh. After a month at Bruck an der Mur, my hometown in Austria, I arrived at Amaravati in October 1992, with a woman from Germany whom I had met in Suan Mokkh. Ajahn Buddhadasa died in summer 1993.

Did you bid farewell to Ajahn Buddhadasa?
No. He was so ill that in the last few weeks of my stay he did not even leave his kuti. I said goodbye to him in my heart. I left some of my possessions with the women who worked in the kitchen, since at the time I was planning to return. I eventually decided not to, although I did visit Suan Mokkh again briefly in 1995.

Your path to Buddhism sounds like an adventure story. You mentioned that you felt as if you were building on previous lives. Does it have to be like this? Is there a simpler way? There are surely people who feel drawn to Buddhism without believing in rebirth or without such strong feelings towards it – for example, because they

have read a particular book. Where does one start? Is there such a thing as a minimalist version of Buddhism?
Of course, it does not have to be the way it was with me. The minimalist version of Buddhism consists of taking refuge and adhering to the five precepts or training rules.

Taking refuge means literally the taking of refuge: taking refuge in the Buddha, in the Dharma, that is, the Buddha's teachings, and in the Sangha, those who have developed insight into reality. These are the ones who are able to guide the wider sangha – the community of people who benefit from the Buddhist teachings, who are convinced that there must be more to life than consuming and enjoying oneself.

The five precepts are: to abstain from killing, to abstain from stealing, to abstain from sexual misconduct, to abstain from lying, and to abstain from consuming drugs and alcohol that could lead to carelessness and thus potentially to the breaking of the other four precepts. In my opinion, if you drink a glass of wine but adhere to the other four precepts you are not breaking a precept. It is about not being careless or negligent. Certain things fall away by themselves when the time is right, even if you cannot imagine it at first.

Does the prohibition on killing mean that one cannot eat meat?
No, it does not mean that literally. It depends entirely how you interpret it – it is up to you. I have never really set out to be a vegetarian in order to be a good nun. Our precepts do not require this either. However, we do have an obligation to accept every meal that is given to us. In Thailand people want to give nuns and monks the best of what they have, and this is often meat, because it is expensive, so these days we

tell people that we are vegetarian. If someone does not know this and brings meat, we eat a small part of it, to show our appreciation, and give the rest away. Make it easy for others to support you – this is an important attitude for monastics who live on alms.

What about moth traps, are these forbidden? It's not as if I am killing animals with my own hands.

Using moth traps is the same as killing moths. We once had a rat infestation at the guest house in Amaravati. After lengthy consideration we decided to call in a professional pest controller. Nobody can make such a difficult decision for you. There is even a chant where you pray that these animals will disappear: all legless, two-legged, four-legged, eight-legged creatures, please go away! You chant this a couple of times and hope for the best, and sometimes it actually works! But if they remain and continue to do damage, something must be done. This is really the last option, and it should only be taken after deep reflection and when all other possibilities have been exhausted.

Can one make amends for such acts?

Yes, one can make amends for everything in the long run. In Buddhism there is no sin in the Christian sense. But everything that you deliberately do, say, or think, whether wholesome or unwholesome, has its effect. That is karma or intentional action. Karma means very simply 'action with intention'.

What were your experiences in Thailand like? Can one tell that the majority of people there are Buddhists?

One cannot really make such generalizations. The majority

of people in Thailand are culturally Buddhist, just like I was culturally Catholic. Buddhism is part of the culture there. People in Thailand have a good understanding of dana – of generosity and giving. The fact that it is a good thing to be generous is deeply rooted in their culture, even for people who do not meditate or adhere to the five precepts.

People who devote themselves to the practice of Buddhism earn respect – at least, the monks do. It is considered commendable to support them. Even someone like my ex-husband, who could not adhere to the five precepts, thought that it would be good to do so and to support monks. Before our wedding he became a monk for a week, a practice that is still expected in a traditional Thai family today.

When I was at school, I remember learning that Buddhism was detached from life because, in Buddhism, life is considered suffering. That is not quite right. With the four noble truths, the Buddha teaches that suffering is caused by attachment, not that life itself is suffering. It is difficult to generalize about how deeply you need to engage, but you need to adhere to the five precepts if you want to progress. Otherwise, you will always take one step forwards and one step back. If you break one of the precepts, you just start again. Making mistakes is part of the training. But we should pay attention to why the lapse occurred.

The practice of Buddhism is less about what happens in your life than about how you relate to what happens. This is very central. Imagine that you want to collect your friend from the station, but it is raining, you get wet, and arrive late. How do you behave, if you are completely soaked and arrive too late? In what mental state do you arrive at the station? That is what is decisive, not the details of what has happened. It is about developing an increasing openness of mind and understanding that one does not need to intervene in everything that happens, that one can give everything the space it needs in order to respond with compassion and wisdom – with respect to the five precepts.

If someone begins to practise Buddhism, are they purposefully aiming for enlightenment from the very beginning?
No. Pushing and forcing is the opposite of letting go, which is why in Buddhism one talks about the middle way. One cannot force the mind to open. It is about looking at oneself again and again, seeing what is happening inside and how one relates to one's own experiences. Buddhist practice actually begins by healing the ego. You can only let go of the ego if it is stable enough in the first place. The ego must be fairly healthy so that you can really practise, so that you can see yourself honestly.

What does this require? How does one recognize this recovery?
When one can adhere to the five precepts without too much difficulty; when one can live in a community without falling victim to one's own projections and constantly arguing with others; when one can live a reasonably balanced life. That is why sangha is so important. One can delude oneself about many things when one is alone. In a community this is harder; in a community one really gets to know oneself.

However, it should ideally be a community of people who are really on the path, a community of people who want to move in a wholesome direction. You are influenced on a daily basis by the energy of the people whom you live with, and there is a chant that recommends not associating with fools. Classical psychology is about healing the ego. However, Buddhism goes further. The ego is seen for what it is – empty. It does not really exist; what you think of and experience as yourself, as a separate person, is actually only a huge pile of thoughts that you more or less cling to. Certain patterns can be discerned in these thoughts, and the ego is the sum of these thought patterns, built up over the course of countless lives, or at least over the course of this life.

You once told me that you quickly feel excluded in social situations. That is one such pattern, and a part of how your ego defines itself. Someone else will be carrying another trauma from their childhood. With the help of Buddhist practice these patterns are consciously recognized and slowly diluted. It is as if you are pouring more and more water onto them. These patterns of attachment are increasingly diluted, until they have completely disappeared.

When was the moment you thought, now I am seeing through the emptiness of the ego, now the practice is starting properly?
That is not how it goes. The practice starts properly at the beginning, not just when you have the first deep insights. It is a process that develops, and over which you have no real control. A hen sits on her eggs and does not know when the chicks will hatch. She broods tirelessly and carries on practising. A carpenter uses his axe every day, and after a couple of years sees that the handle is worn and that he can see the imprints of his fingers. He does not know when this happened. Five, four, or three years ago? Yesterday? It

happened over the course of time. It is the same with Buddhist practice. The longer one practises, the easier it is to let go of striving towards a goal. At some point one realizes that it does not work like this, and then one begins to relax.

The practice of Buddhism is not linear. There is a lovely saying: the shortest distance between two points is not always a straight line. If you keep at it, if you realize that you cannot control how the process develops, then your initial struggle will turn into devotion. What you have control over is whether you make an effort to set and live by wise priorities. Through daily practice and by adhering to the five precepts you can cultivate a solid basis for your journey.

Finding the Middle Way

You are sitting here before me with your head shaved, dressed in a red-brown robe. Which school of Buddhism do you belong to?
My outward appearance and the way I live correspond to Theravada Buddhism. The monasteries in Thailand and the United Kingdom, where I trained, belong to the Thai Forest Tradition. I live as a bhikkhuni, which is the highest level of ordination for women in all three schools of Buddhism. Men are known as bhikkhus. I am also influenced by Shechen Rabjam Rinpoche, my teacher from the Nyingma tradition[9] of Tibetan Buddhism. His teaching opened up many things for me at that time that I could not find in Theravada.

What are the major traditions within Buddhism, and how do they differ from each other?
Popular classification distinguishes between Theravada Buddhism – also known as the 'School of the Elders', which is based on the Pali Canon[10] – Mahayana Buddhism, and Vajrayana Buddhism, that is, Tibetan Buddhism. However, this division into three major schools is being increasingly questioned. It was long assumed that these schools were established one after another, but this may not actually have been the case.

Contemporary scholars have started to compare the earliest materials from the different schools with each other, and have found common elements in Pali, Chinese, and Tibetan sources. Today the expression 'Early Buddhism' is becoming increasingly accepted: this encapsulates the essence of the teachings that were taught by the Buddha himself when he lived on Earth more than 2,500 years ago. One can narrow these down with relative certainty using comparative research.

Over the course of history, such different forms of expression of the Buddha's teachings developed in Tibet, China, and Japan that at first glance it is hard to see that they are all about the same thing. The first Europeans who travelled to Asia did not understand that this was all Buddhism; they thought that they were looking at quite different religions.

At meetings or conferences, it is usually not hard to find a common denominator. The four noble truths are called 'the elephant's footprint'. All of the different teachings of Buddhism fit inside the footprint of the largest animal. If there is something that does not fit, that is not Buddhism.

The essential points of Buddhism actually fit onto a postcard. The four noble truths could be summed up as follows: There is suffering or stress. What is the reason for the stress? Attachment, and the remedy is letting go. For this there is the noble eightfold path, *ariya atthangika magga*, which makes letting go possible through understanding:

- right view
- right intention
- right speech
- right action
- right livelihood

- right effort
- right mindfulness
- right stability/collectedness.

The noble eightfold path does not envisage linear progress – all the elements are deeply interwoven. For example, right intention is also connected to the other seven parts of the path, like a rope that is woven from eight strands that all work together. The noble eightfold path can be divided into three groups: the first group deals with wisdom, *panna*; the second, ethics, *sila*; and the third, collectedness or meditation, *samadhi*.

Different cultures have used different ways and means to communicate this essence. It can all seem a little strange to a European, if one does not explain what it is all about.

Could you say which school of Buddhism is the easiest for Europeans to understand?
That is hard to say if a person does not know what they may have practised in previous lives. With Ajahn Buddhadasa in Thailand I started to meditate in the Thai Forest Tradition. In the first weeks my mind was flooded with images from the Vajrayana. But I am from Bruck an der Mur in Styria, Austria! Looking back, I would say that these images were probably already in my subconscious from previous lives. They were activated through the whole environment and through the stimuli that I received at Ajahn Buddhadasa's monastery.

For someone else it might be strange, confusing, or even frightening to enter a Vajrayana shrine room for the first time. In Tibet, two very different traditions, shamanism and Buddhism, flowed into each other, and gave birth to this unbelievable exuberance of forms.

The simplicity and clarity of the Theravada teachings are a very good basis to start from. One observes one's own mind, learns how it works and how one can steer it in a wholesome direction through training. The first step is therefore to observe oneself. In doing so one will see things that one cannot resolve by oneself, things that can only be resolved in a relationship – with a teacher. Without basic training, a 'resting in oneself', a certain understanding of how one works, where one's own strengths and weaknesses lie, one is not really in a position to make use of more complex instruction.

In Vajrayana Buddhism there is something called 'skilful means'. How should I think of this? Can you give me an example?
All schools of Buddhism refer to skilful means; in fact, the whole body of teachings can be seen as a collection of such skilful means. Skilful means are there to dissolve certain filters and are tailored to your particular personality.

At the start of my Buddhist practice I had no idea about anything. I never spoke with my first teacher, Ajahn Buddhadasa. Many things were transmitted without words, from heart to heart or from mind to mind. This can happen between a teacher and a disciple if there is good resonance. Tibetan Buddhism created the so-called sadhanas from this possibility. A whole world of experience is built around one particular deity: there is a visualization, prayers, mantras,[11] followed by an empowerment that takes place by visualizing rays of light. At the end, this mental construct is dissolved. In doing this, one thing becomes clear through repetition: everything is empty. Something is built up, then it is used as a skilful means, and at the end it is dissolved.

In this way, through practice, the whole world becomes increasingly understood and perceived as constantly dissolving or being in constant flux. The skilful means are methods of bringing this truth closer to oneself. In all practice it is important not to get lost in a fascination for exotic forms and unusual situations, or to use these as an escape from the spiritual work that takes place internally.

For example, in Theravada Buddhism you focus on your breath when you are meditating. The mind wanders off again and again, and you bring it back. When you work with your breathing like this, it will eventually sink in: everything is constantly changing. This is what it is really about: fully comprehending that everything that comes into being will also pass. That is the gateway to liberation.

The principles that must be understood in order to free oneself from limiting patterns of thought and behaviour are actually really simple: the first is impermanence, the transience of all phenomena that arise and pass away. In the Pali Canon this is described as *anicca*. The second is unsatisfactoriness, *dukkha*. Nothing, at the end of the day, is capable of providing permanent satisfaction. Everything arises and passes away, and this is outside our control. The recording device for our conversation, which is lying on the table here, is very satisfactory for you at the moment, but at some point it will no longer be. The third principle that must be understood is emptiness, not-self, or *anatta*, as it is called in the Pali Canon. This principle points to the fact that all constantly changing things are not things that exist separately, but instead are deeply interdependent processes. This recording device is made up of many parts. But, whatever those parts are, the whole universe is involved, since they are made of stardust that came into being billions of years ago.

This is not really complicated. The important thing, however, is to remember this when emotions run high, because that is when one needs this kind of knowledge – this is what the practice is actually all about. All schools of Buddhism attempt to explain this in their own way. But these are simply different approaches based on different cultures.

What cultural characteristics does Theravada Buddhism have?
Theravada Buddhism is also called Southern Buddhism. It spread from India to Sri Lanka, Thailand, Myanmar, Laos, and Cambodia. People say that, a long time ago, all three schools – Theravada, Mahayana, and Vajrayana – coexisted on the Malaysian Peninsula, all the way down to Borneo.

The Borobudur Temple of the Mahayana School, the largest Buddhist monument in the world, is in Borneo. In Ajahn Buddhadasa's hometown in Chaiya in South Thailand, a statue of Avalokiteshvara, the bodhisattva of compassion in Mahayana Buddhism, was excavated. There is a copy of it at the Suan Mokkh monastery. The boundaries between the different schools were not always so exact: teachers and monastics travelled and passed on the teachings wherever they went.

Thailand is the only country in South-East Asia that was never formally colonized. This was due, among other things, to the reforms carried out by King Chulalongkorn, who reigned until the early twentieth century. He attempted to eliminate shamanistic elements and ancestor worship from Buddhism in order to pre-empt Western criticism. Ajahn Buddhadasa continued this later: the attempt to demonstrate that Buddhism can be reconciled with science and modern insights. Buddhism was thus already 'modernized' more than a hundred years ago, before it became more broadly accessible in the West.

The first people to bring Buddhism to the West travelled mainly in countries where Theravada Buddhism was prevalent. In 1940 a German musician became a Buddhist monk in what was then Ceylon, today Sri Lanka, and took the name Nyanatiloka. He compiled a German-language dictionary of Buddhist terms[12] that is still in use today.

As a practising Buddhist, what is special about this school for you?
To answer your question, I would like to talk not about Theravada but about Early Buddhism. Bhikkhu Anālayo, a German scholar and Buddhist monk, has become well known through his research in this field. He knows Tibetan, Chinese, Pali, and other languages, and is thus in a position to compare the written records of the different schools. Early Buddhism puts the minimum that one must work with in order to free the mind and heart at its very centre. This is the basic template for a successful practice – less than this is not possible.

For example, the thirty-seven *bodhipakkhiya-dhamma*[13] – the thirty-seven qualities that inspire awakening – belong to these very early teachings. The things that are discussed here were later expanded significantly in Mahayana and Vajrayana Buddhism. The seven awakening factors (*bojjhanga*) are a subset of the *bodhipakkiya-dhamma*:

- mindfulness (*sati*)
- investigation (*dhammavicaya*)
- energy (*viriya*)

- joy (*piti*)
- tranquillity (*passaddhi*)
- stability/collectedness (*samadhi*)
- equipoise (*upekkha*).

The seven awakening factors belong to the core elements of the teaching, just like the five hindrances:

- sensual desire
- ill will
- sloth and torpor
- restlessness and worry
- doubt.

One strives to transform these hindrances and, in so doing, cultivates the awakening factors. When the mind is fully freed from these limitations, then the awakening factors are in full bloom. This is awakening.

Are there different paths of practice within Theravada Buddhism?
In Theravada there have always been three different paths: the path of the arahant, the path of the buddha, and the path of the pacceka buddha. An arahant is free of all mental delusions and has gone beyond rebirth in any form. There is no more wanting and doing; an arahant is like a flame that is extinguished when the fuel has run out. In Theravada there is also the buddha path: one strives to become a buddha, a completely and perfectly awakened one (Pali: *sammasambuddha*). There are two different buddhas on the buddha path: the buddha and the pacceka buddha. The latter is a buddha who does not have the gift of teaching, sometimes also described as a 'silent buddha'.

In Mahayana Buddhism we find the so-called bodhisattva vow – whoever takes this vow does not strive towards the complete extinguishing of the flame by letting go of all action and volition. In order to serve all sentient beings, a bodhisattva instead aims to be reborn again and again, until all sentient beings have been freed. In Mahayana Buddhism it is therefore considered selfish to practise the arahant path.

Unfortunately, in some Buddhist circles people still speak of 'Hinayana', literally the 'small vehicle', when they refer to Theravada Buddhism. This is derogatory. What is meant is that only one person can fit inside the small vehicle, and therefore this practice can only be used to solve one's own problems. Mahayana Buddhists, by contrast, take the bodhisattva vow and promise to practise for the benefit of others.

However, I can see no real contradiction here. When something is truly wholesome for oneself, truly wholesome in a comprehensive sense, then it is also beneficial for others. This is a central assertion in the Pali Canon: if you do something that is really good for you in the long term, then it is also good for everyone else in the long term. One should keep the consequences of one's own thoughts, one's own words, and one's own deeds in mind at all times.

In the more than thirty years that I have been a practising Buddhist, it has become increasingly clear to me that the teachings of the different schools of Buddhism are essentially the same, even though culturally they seem very different. After such a long time I find it hard to commit to one particular way. In my practice I take the middle path in this respect too and am open to teachings from different schools of Buddhism. All schools of Buddhism offer a deep insight into the Dhamma (Pali) or Dharma (Sanskrit), the teachings of the Buddha.

These teachings can permanently cut through ignorance and the ties that bind us to rebirth. When you understand which insights are needed to break through ignorance, then you have arrived at the essence of Buddhism. The knife – in a figurative sense – that we need to cut through the bonds of ignorance can take different forms, depending on whether we are in Senegal, in the Tyrol, or in Nepal. The important thing is that we can cut things with it and sharpen it. That is what makes a knife.

Is the expression 'religion' actually appropriate for Buddhism?
First you would have to define the word 'religion'. For me the word is associated with the Latin *religare*, which means 'to tie back, to bind or bind tightly'. It is all about connecting to the whole, to the universe, and experiencing a sense of being part of something greater than oneself. Or however we want to express that which cannot really be grasped by language. Some people call it God, while in Buddhism we call it Dhamma or Dharma. In essence it is that which cannot really be named. We know that we are a part of it; the more one experiences oneself as a part of it, the less one is afraid and the more content one is in life.

I get the impression that Buddhists need to work very hard on themselves. By contrast, Christianity, as I experienced it in my childhood, is quite simple for the individual: you need to be faithful, go to church regularly, and follow the Ten Commandments. Isn't that a trifle compared with what is required of you in Buddhism?
Not really. Christian mystics like Master Eckhart or Teresa of Avila probably had similar insights to the ones I mentioned

earlier. It is a question of the maturity of the practitioner. A question of spiritual maturity – whether you are ready to open yourself to the possibility that God is not human, not a father-figure, but rather a mystery. For us Buddhists, the laws of nature come closest to this. Dharma can be thought of as the natural laws that underpin reality. Take climate change, for example. Science claims to have understood much for many centuries, but it hasn't really, since humanity is currently still much too focused on itself. We look at the universe and believe we know our way around, just because we have developed such powerful machines. In reality, however, we do not really understand what is actually going on.

Healing and Moving Forward

We have been friends for more than forty years. I have observed profound changes in you since you began to practise Buddhism. Would you say that, for you, Buddhism is a path of healing?
Definitely: every spiritual path is. It offers healing from ignorance or delusion.

How would you explain delusion to a non-Buddhist?
Greed, hatred, aversion, jealousy... these states of mind are expressions of delusion. People are usually concerned with wanting more of one particular thing or less of another. Holding on or pushing away, not wanting to have – both of these patterns are variants of attachment. Attachment distorts reality, since it is an attempt to stop a flow. If you stand in an actual river and attempt to stop the flow of water, pressure builds up. The water begins to swirl around and is no longer on its natural course. This leads to a distortion of what is really there.

In Early Buddhism one speaks of the four *vipallasa*, the four distortions of perception:

- seeing what is impermanent (*anicca*) as permanent (*nicca*)
- seeing what is painful (*dukkha*) as pleasant (*sukha*)
- seeing what is without a self (*anatta*) as a self (*atta*)

- seeing what is not beautiful (*asubha*) as beautiful (*subha*).

Can you give a concrete example from your own development to illustrate liberation from delusion and attachment?
I have developed more trust in the flow of life as it is. I am aware of the lure of consumer society, but at the same time there are many things I no longer get involved with. It is clearer to me than ever that my contentment and the subtle joy that it brings do not come from the things I possess. You can own the most amazing things and still be desperately unhappy. I have fewer needs and thus more freedom. Buddhist practice promises freedom from attachment and thus freedom from mental delusions and the resulting distortions.

If you apply this to your everyday life then you have less stress in the here and now. You feel less pressure to earn a particular level of income in order to be able to buy all these things whose importance is drummed into you by the advertising industry.

You spoke about attachments that should be overcome. I can also become attached to things that cost nothing – for example, I can take pleasure in a butterfly or a flower.
Of course, you can take pleasure in the butterfly and the flower and therefore do not need to become attached.

For me it is difficult to tell the difference. People say that Buddhism turns away from life in the here and now, since life is suffering, and turns towards another dimension.
This is a wrong interpretation or translation, from the time when Buddhism was first encountered by the West. The expression

dukkha was translated as 'suffering'. However, *dukkha* actually means 'unsatisfactory'. The word *dukkha* consists of two parts: *du* is a negative word and means something like 'not fitting', while *kha* describes the hole in the middle of a wheel, into which the axle is inserted. If the axle does not fit into the hole, the wheel will wobble, and it will be a bumpy journey. That is what dukkha actually means. And this unsatisfactory quality is not inherent in phenomena themselves – rather it is the result of particular expectations regarding such phenomena.

There is nothing that can satisfy you in the long term. This recording device, this chair, and everything else in this room will at some point break and stop working. All things are unsatisfactory, so you cannot base your happiness on a thing or on another person. Of course you can enjoy everything in the moment, as long as it gives you pleasure, but, if possible, do so without becoming attached to it, if you want to avoid the resulting stress that this brings.

The four noble truths are often compared to the diagnosis of a doctor. The Buddha can be seen as a spiritual doctor who can heal the illness of delusion. At the start the diagnosis is that there is dukkha or the experience of suffering. A mind that is not fully awakened attaches to things, resulting in stress and suffering. Every person who lives with a little mindfulness will see that everything in life is constantly changing. Therefore there is nothing that can satisfy you permanently – that is the first realization. To live is to experience discomfort. We cannot really control our own lives.

The second truth concerns the origin of dukkha. What is the germ, the pathogen that has caused this illness? It is attachment. Attachment and suffering or stress arise simultaneously: inadequacy is not a quality inherent in phenomena, but rather a result of attachment.

The third truth is an answer to the question about what constitutes a realistic and healthy condition. It means seeing things as they really are, without becoming attached to them. This is freedom from dukkha.

The fourth truth is the noble eightfold path: the treatment plan for achieving the third noble truth, health, by truly following the doctor's prescription.

So there is no contradiction between Buddhism and the joy of living?
No, none at all. Joy is, after all, one of the seven awakening factors:[14] without joy there is no awakening. One can also experience joy without attachment, that is, joy in the moment. Yesterday I was sitting in my friend's garden when a huge flock of starlings suddenly flew over us. I heard the beating of their wings and felt a deep happiness. And then they were gone. That is true joy – in the moment. You can be happy and grateful to be able to experience something like this, without necessarily hoping that it will come back soon.

If I have no attachment, am I automatically living in the moment?
Yes, and this leads to a quite different quality of joy, a subtle joy that is not based on the senses. If you contemplate this with a clouded mind, then you will most likely not be able to understand it. If you experience some kind of sensory pleasure and at the same time worry that it will pass, that is not actual joy.

Such an attitude is marked by fear, and this fear blocks the path to true happiness. If you are in the flow of life, then enjoyable things will surface again and again. Joyful moments will occur, even if you are very ill or poor.

When I think of the impermanence of all things it brings me to a dilemma. In the long term everything will dissolve and we will all return to dust. Our human species will disappear from the planet, other species will come, and at some point the sun will go out. Why should I bother making any effort? For example, for the sake of social justice, the climate crisis, or biodiversity?

When your mother is ill, you don't say 'I don't need to look after her since she's going to die one day anyway.' If that was our attitude, we could all annihilate ourselves straight away. As long as we can, and out of kindness, it is always appropriate to try to alleviate suffering. This also corresponds to the four divine abidings (*brahmavihara*), which are so important in Buddhism and which are also called the four immeasurables:

- loving-kindness (*metta*)
- compassion (*karuna*)
- gladness (*mudita*)
- equanimity (*upekkha*).

Having equanimity in the face of what takes place in the world is often misunderstood. Equanimity does not mean not caring, but has a lot to do with courage.

You are open to everything, even if it is frightening or too exciting. You always have the same courage to say: yes, I can engage with this. That is a central part of the Buddha's teachings – to recognize how you relate to your own experience. You cannot change the natural laws, but, to the extent that it is viable, you can muster the greatest possible goodness and kindness and carry on practising. In doing so you are also doing yourself a favour, since you are training your mind positively and thus reducing your ego. When you die, these mental habits will have a good influence on your next birth. You are the greatest beneficiary, and, at the same time, it is also good for others or for the person you are looking after. In this way every situation in life can be our teacher.

In Buddhism people are always talking about practice. What is this actually? What is the minimum I can do and still say, I am a Buddhist? What must I think, what must I believe, what must I do?
In any event you must endeavour to adhere to the five precepts that we have already discussed. Naturally there will always be lapses, but when these occur you open yourself to any feelings of remorse and immediately start again. There can be no discussion about this. A second basis for calling yourself a Buddhist is the three refuges. These do not necessarily need to be taken in a formal ceremony, but you should at least work in this general direction.

Can you explain 'refuges'?
Imagine a storm is raging and everyone is afraid. Instead of standing outside in the middle of the snowstorm, you decide to take refuge in a hut. A Buddhist takes refuge in the Buddha, the Dharma, and the Sangha.

She takes refuge in the Buddha who left us these teachings. On another level she also takes refuge in the inner buddha, mindfulness or awareness. Buddha is awareness itself or the historical Buddha or both. The Buddha stands for the perfection of awareness. He is someone who has completely perfected awareness or mindfulness, and we are still on our way, although we have the same potential as him. One day we will get there too, but, for now, we are where we are.

Dharma is the teaching that you find in the Buddhist texts, but also laws such as those concerning how nature, the mind, and dependent origination work. Dharma is also the different lists, commentaries, and everything else that countless people have used to attempt to explain this teaching in such a way that others can understand it.

Sangha, the third object of refuge in Buddhism, includes not only its teachers, but in the wider sense also those sitting next to you when you meditate – all of those who practise Buddhism, who feel connected to it, and who have benefited from these teachings. Those who have attained some level of realization are called the Ariya Sangha.

Someone who has sought refuge knows that a storm is raging and that she is sometimes afraid. She asks herself how best to continue. She uses all these elements to reach the best possible decision. Someone who has not really understood how to take refuge in the Buddha or in awareness will panic and get lost in their fear.

What does realization mean in this context?
Realization means that you have truly seen the Dharma at least once. You have actually understood or realized emptiness through direct seeing or through your own experience. In Early Buddhism one speaks of the ten fetters that bind us to the wheel of rebirth. This is one method used for explaining the delusions that cloud the mind. As I have already said, Buddhist practice is about gradually dissolving these delusions. In Theravada Buddhism, the first of the four stages

of realization or awakening is entering the stream. A stream-enterer is someone who has entered the stream of the Dharma. They no longer need a teacher, and only need to take care that they do not get caught on either bank but keep returning to the middle and continuing to flow with the stream. Through the first deep realization of emptiness, the first three fetters that bind one to the wheel of rebirth are permanently broken.

Breaking the first three fetters means no longer having any doubt concerning the efficacy of the teachings, because one has experienced it oneself. It also means no longer believing that following particular rites and rituals precisely will have a liberating effect. They can be supportive, in providing the mind with joy and motivation, but the rituals themselves cannot free you. Breaking the third fetter means no longer believing that you are a separate being. One still continues to experience oneself like this, but, as soon as one reflects on it, one sees that one does not contain an immutable core that one could point to and say, this is me, this is my self. There is nothing permanent there, only patterns of thought and the body, which will return to the elements after death. Then there are three further stages of realization, up to arahant, full awakening.

So, you can measure your progress in Buddhist practice?
Yes, even without describing these fetters so precisely, I would observe: I have less fear, I have more joy, more trust in life. I need fewer things. I can climb back out of patterns of thought that I fall into. Everyone can ascertain this for themselves, and sometimes we can also observe this in others to a certain extent.

Is there such a thing as spiritual ambition?
This is inevitable when the ego is still large enough. It is better than not caring at all, but ambition can also be counterproductive. Making too much effort is the opposite of letting go. The point is to metaphorically discard baggage. If you start off with ten suitcases, put three away, and carry on with seven, then you have admittedly lightened your load to a certain extent, but it would be ridiculous to make a big deal about it. In order to be able to know whether someone else has entered the stream, you need to have come at least that far yourself. In order to know whether someone is a buddha, you need to be a buddha yourself.

How can I recognize my own progress? Or is this irrelevant?
No, it is very important. But progress here is not the same as with other projects one works on in life. Often there is progress when one gives up, when one believes one simply cannot go on. One gives it all up and puts it to one side and then suddenly, when one is in the shower, insight arrives. Naturally the groundwork was an essential part of it.

Many people like me start to meditate, then give up for long periods, before starting again. Is there progress in this situation, or is all the effort pointless if I do not practise consistently and regularly?
It is never pointless, but it is hard to generalize. Your spiritual development does not depend only on how much energy you put into your practice in this life. It also depends on how much merit you have accumulated in previous lives, and which qualities of the heart and mind you were born with this time around.

Are you saying that we never start from zero?
No, we do not start our life with an empty page. Someone might meditate five times and then enter the stream. I have frequently heard teachers say that people in Asia have more faith and place more trust in the teachings. And there is great respect there for Buddhist clergy, for cultural reasons, particularly among people in rural areas. For example, if a rice farmer goes to a teacher, and the teacher tells him, 'Stop thinking and simply watch your breathing!', then he will just do that. He is capable of doing that and can make enormous progress. Meanwhile, someone else, for example, a university professor from the United States who knows all the Buddhist books by heart, will sit down and despair over his complex mind. And, at some point, he will give up, and maybe it will happen then. But the rice farmer might already have made a hundred times as much progress. He does not doubt the instructions, and applies them one after another. You never know which doors will open to you, but it is always very helpful to spend time with someone who is already ahead of you. If I had not spent so much time with Ajahn Buddhadasa, who knows whether I would have had the stamina to follow the path that opened to me. When I came to the monastery and became a postulant, I tried out various forms of practice, including the jhanas or immersions. These are different levels of concentration that are often mentioned in the Buddhist texts. However, this was not quite the appropriate approach for me, and over the years my practice has actually become gradually simpler.

It took me a while to find my own path, but I did not give up straight away when things did not go as I had imagined. I always knew that at some point I would find what was right for me. I do not know where this confidence came from. When one considers practice as something that is spread out over several lives – which in fact it is – then one does not really need to agonize over it. It will all come together at some point.

We have already spoken about the fundamentals of Buddhist practice: taking refuge and the five precepts. What else belongs to Buddhist practice?

The five precepts are very realistic and far-reaching if you really integrate them into your life. They apply not only when you are at the meditation centre, but also when you are at work or when you go shopping, simply all the time.

Naturally, meditation is part of practice too. Without the cultivation of mindfulness and awareness, it does not work. You will not be able to adhere even to the five precepts if you do not have a certain level of mindfulness. In the same way that, if you want to train your muscles, you will need certain equipment, it is difficult to train mindfulness without meditation. You do not necessarily need to meditate by sitting down cross-legged; you can also train your mind without adopting this posture, although this posture has stood the test of time. When the body is resting in a stable, grounded position, it is much easier to direct awareness towards the mind.

What if I don't want to change my work and my family life, but want to intensify my practice?

Then you need to look at your daily life and consider what you can do without in order to create more time for meditation. You can change your priorities. For example, you could meditate instead of watching television and decide to go to sleep an hour earlier. Then you can get up an hour earlier the next day in order to meditate before your day begins. One can always make time for practice if one really wants to.

Are there any methods for reaching one's goal more quickly?
Every teacher will say, 'my method!', because these are the methods that have worked for them.

And what if I asked you as a friend and teacher?
Then I would say this: listen to your inner guidance and discuss it with someone experienced whom you trust. Perhaps you are not being honest with yourself; if so, it would be good to be challenged by someone who already knows how it goes. It is important to keep asking yourself: what would be important to me if I were to die now? This helps to set priorities, but it does not mean giving up your obligations towards your family and your children. That would clearly not be wholesome conduct.

So, we are standing at the starting line with different handicaps, varying levels of fitness, with different amounts of luggage, and in different shoes. And presumably our goal is enlightenment?
Awakening would be a better word. Awakening means no longer being attached to joys, fears, and hopes, and instead being fully immersed in the stream of life and totally open to life, as it is. One cannot imagine this; one can only experience it directly in the moment. However, there are signposts – for example, when one observes oneself and sees how the mind clings to things and what effect this has. As soon as you have entered the stream you cease to have any doubt that it is possible.

However, until this has taken place, the doubt will keep coming back. For this reason, it is helpful to surround yourself with people who are more advanced than you. You listen to teachings, you ask questions, you put photos of your teachers on your shrine. You get a blessing; you get a refuge name and a blessing cord. All of these skilful means will help you to maintain your trust and your faith that you will manage this path. Until you have fully realized it yourself, and then you do not need all this anymore.

The teachings are sometimes compared to a raft that we need in order to reach the other shore. Once we are finished with it, we can simply leave it behind, because its work is done. We do not need to carry the raft along with us anymore.

How much effort does it take to reach the point where you enter the stream?
This is not so easy to say, since it depends how and where one begins. If you compare it with music, one person might start as a little Mozart with a natural talent, while another might at first seem to be completely tone-deaf. And yet the one with less natural talent might have unlimited trust, when the teacher tells him something, because he has no preconceptions. This does not have to be a disadvantage.

Entering the stream affects your future rebirths; it is said that, after entering the stream, you are reborn up to seven times in the human realm or as a higher being but no longer as an animal, a hell being, or a hungry ghost.

Rebirths and realms are quite tricky concepts for non-Buddhists to get their heads around. How can they be explained simply?
Two key expressions from the Buddha's teachings are samsara and nirvana. 'Samsara' can be translated as the cycle of existence or of rebirths. Existence is seen as a restless sea that

ceaselessly surges up and down. All beings are caught in an apparently irresolvable process of repeated rebirth, ageing, illness, and death.

Nirvana is extinguishment, the exit from this cycle of existence, and the goal of Buddhist practice. Samsara is a view of the world and not a place itself: the 'un-awakened' or unenlightened perspective on the world and life. Will and action are always at work, which is also the reason we experience suffering and unsatisfactoriness.

Take, for example, a pair of reading glasses. They are not inadequate in and of themselves, but, if I want them to last forever and to adapt to my eyesight as it changes with age, then I will experience the unsatisfactoriness of these glasses. This is because I want the glasses to be something other than what they actually are and can be for me. Samsara can be explained like this.

However, when all greed, aversion, and delusion are washed out of the 'river of consciousness', the same situation will be experienced as nirvana, since the perspective on things will be in harmony with how they really are.

In Buddhism one recognizes the six realms of existence in which one may be reborn in accordance with one's intentional actions in previous lives: the hell realm, the hungry-ghost realm, the animal realm, the human realm, the asura or jealous-gods realm, and the heavenly realm.

There are two possible interpretations: you can take these realms to be actual places where you come into being or are born, or you can imagine yourself being born into these realms countless times each day, that is, you can take them as being concerned purely with mental and emotional experiences.

According to this second interpretation, someone addicted to drugs would spend a large part of his day in the hungry-ghost realm. Then, when he is full of drugs, he might be in the realm of heavenly beings for one or two hours, until the drugs wear off, plunging him down into the hell realm. During a delicious meal we are in heaven for a moment, but ten hours later we are hungry again, and this keeps on repeating forever. However, it is possible to climb out of this apparently endless cycle.

How does one get out of these realms?
Through insight. People say that you have the best preconditions for Buddhist practice if you are born in the human realm. In the human realm there is generally speaking some kind of balance between pain and pleasure. In our realm we are not constantly under stress because we do not have enough, unlike the hungry ghosts. The animal realm is ruled by fear, and in hell there is so much pain and suffering that there is not enough space around experience, and thus no progress in the direction of liberation is possible.

In the realm of the asuras, total distraction reigns due to constant power struggles, and for heavenly beings it is so comfortable that there is no incentive for Buddhist practice at all. For this reason, people say that it is very important to make full use of the chance of having been born human. For someone who has not entered the stream, there is no guarantee that they will be born in the human realm again.

So, to sum up, the minimum requirements for a Buddhist are observing the five precepts, taking refuge, and practising, that is, meditating and cultivating mindfulness and awareness.
Yes, that is right.

What is the fundamental difference between the path as a Buddhist nun and the path as a layperson?
There is no fundamental difference. Rules, taking refuge, and training in mindfulness: for me as a nun it is more intense – I simply adopt more rules. We could describe full ordination as a voluntary straitjacket that turns into an anchor over the course of the years – an anchor that secures our own expression of the Dharma and eventually makes it truly effective.

For me the flame under my cooking pot is turned up a little higher perhaps – otherwise our practice is based on the same four noble truths, whether I am a nun or a layperson. I have spent more than thirty years living in monastic communities and learned what kind of support is required to be able to observe the rules in a straightforward way. There is also more time spent in meditation in the daily life of a monastery.

Is there such a thing as vows?
We have no vows. We speak about rules or training rules: these are set out in a handbook called the Patimokkha. In it there are four classes of rules – at the highest level, *parajika*, there are eight for nuns and four for monks. If I break one of the rules from the highest level, then I am no longer a bhikkhuni. Even if I do not take off my robes, I am no longer a bhikkhuni in the karmic sense.

Have you ever regretted becoming a nun?
No, I have never regretted it. It has always been clear to me that, if and when I no longer want this kind of life, I will simply stop. In order to do so, I only need one person who understands what I want to say. After I have spoken the sentence, 'I give up my training as a bhikkhuni' three times,

I simply change my clothes and that is that. I can even get ordained again later, although not as a bhikkhuni, but as a samaneri, that is, a novice.

In the Theravada you can become a monk or a nun for a couple of days. For example, if your grandmother dies, you can offer the merit accumulated by your temporary ordination for her onward journey into the next life. These are cultural traditions. My ex-husband also became a monk for a week before our wedding, since it was supposed to be good for the marriage, although it did not help us at all.

What is your obligation to society?
I trained in the Forest Tradition – we are contemplative, and we teach. People can live with us in the community if they are in a position to participate in the daily schedule of the monastery. In Asia, monks and sometimes nuns go into the village early in the morning to collect alms. This is a service that gives householders the opportunity, even before they start work, to take positive actions and acquire merit without having to go to the monastery. At the same time, the monks and nuns are provided with their daily food.

For example, if we go to the local farmers' market, we simply stand there with our bowls and offer people an opportunity to give. The system of almsgiving is also a control mechanism, since it guarantees that monks and nuns can only exist in places where they are valued and thus supported by the surrounding community. The lay supporters provide the four requisites: food, clothing, shelter, and mej104dicine. The members of the monastic community, the samanas, make sure that the Buddha's teachings are passed on and help in many spheres of life, give advice, and perform ceremonies. There is a mutual give and take, like in every other religion.

Is it true that you are not allowed to touch or own any money?
If an elderly woman were to drop a note on the floor and could not bend down to pick it up, I would touch it. It is not about not touching, it is about not controlling money. I cannot have a bank account in my name or buy something without an intermediary. When my father died, I inherited some money that my brother keeps in a trust for me. The money is there to support my practice, to travel and see a teacher, or to pay for books or a particular medicine.

I know Buddhist nuns and monks who gifted a lot of money to their monasteries. These funds were used to pay for houses, land, and extensive building refurbishments. I would like to tell any women who are considering training in a monastery the following: do not burn your bridges, do not give away your savings for the time being. Wait for five or ten years, and see if that is what you really want to do. At the beginning everything looks so rosy, but later things can sometimes develop quite differently.

Money clearly has an important function. We do not believe that we can live without money, but we have a different relationship to money compared with most people.

Practising Emptiness

I think I am not alone if I say that the concept of rebirth – at least in the West – requires some explanation. And it seems to occur right at the beginning of the Buddhist path. Do I have to believe in rebirth in order to be a Buddhist?

No. There are many lay Buddhists who find it hard to get used to the concept of rebirth. One can simply leave the question open by saying: I do not believe in it – I am not saying that it is not true, but I simply do not know. Personally, I have never had any doubt about rebirth. At Wat Suan Mokkh they did not talk about rebirth right at the start. It was a progressive monastery where an attempt was made to present the Buddha's teachings in such a way that people from the West felt drawn to it. The intention was to convey Buddhist concepts without a lot of cultural baggage.

If people ask me what kind of Buddhism I practise, I could say that I cannot and need not decide. Every approach has its own strengths. My Buddhist practice is tailored to my current needs. It is the appropriate medicine for my mind and in keeping with Early Buddhism, the core teachings that underpin all schools of Buddhism.

There are Buddhist teachers like, for example, the former Buddhist monk Stephen Batchelor, who writes extensively about how the belief in rebirth is cultural baggage and actually has no place in modern Buddhism.

For me, believing in rebirth is a major incentive to practise. It makes it clear that I cannot escape my problems. I cannot simply get out of the whole process just because I want to. That is what rebirth means. The mental delusions I do not want to work on, which I do not resolve, will need to be resolved later. If I only clean my room in ten years' time, it will contain ten years' worth of dirt. If I clean it now, however, there will be significantly less.

I can understand that it is an incentive. But isn't the whole of Buddhist teaching built on the idea of wanting to escape the cycle of rebirth? You have to believe that in order to be a Buddhist, don't you?

You can go to the gym with the goal of building the very strongest muscles that a person can develop, or you might just want to be a bit stronger so that you can lift your own boxes next time you move house. You do not necessarily need to follow the teachings all the way to complete awakening; you will already have some benefit when you can deal with your emotions more skilfully.

Perhaps you are starting your practice because you want to have less stress in your life or want to make fewer mistakes in your social environment. This can be at least a provisional goal: you simply do it so that you feel better. Then you notice that the teaching works, and slowly but surely you want to find out more. A year, and then another year goes by... and, at some point, you are in the flow – your entry into practice can be quite gradual.

Do I not need to strive for complete awakening or for an escape from the cycle of rebirth, in order to be considered a Buddhist?
No. And, in any event, it doesn't matter whether someone considers you a Buddhist or not. The Buddha was not a Buddhist either. All of that only came later, but some people find it useful, at least at the start of their practice.

When I returned to Austria from Thailand in 1989, I registered as a Buddhist with the Austrian Buddhist Union in Vienna. I received a piece of paper saying that Sylvia Bayer is a Buddhist. At the time this helped me, but now it does not bother me particularly who considers me to be what.

As I have already mentioned, as a Buddhist one is encouraged to practise the essential requirements, that is, the five precepts and the three refuges. They serve as a sort of GPS in your life. Let us suppose you are travelling on foot from Vienna to Kathmandu. The GPS will tell you the direction you need to walk in. You may not get there in this life, but that does not matter. The main thing is that you are moving in the direction of Kathmandu, not Amsterdam. You go as far as you can, and if, in this example, we equate Kathmandu with complete awakening, you might get stranded in Kabul. This is already quite far, but it is not Kathmandu.

Imagine a candle that has almost burned down, and, before it goes out, you light a new candle from its flame. Is this the same flame as that from the previous candle or not? It is not the same flame, and yet not a different one either. If something is reborn, it is the dynamic or the impulse of the burning itself.

If you imagine a stream, then it is the current of the stream that is reborn. The impulse to flow just keeps on finding a different setting, a different host, a different body. One person wants to become a bodhisattva, and someone else wants to steal the crown jewels. Both of these are 'desires', but it is a different quality of desire, and the ethical quality of this desire determines where the rebirth will take place. That is not too hard to understand, is it?

No, it is not hard to understand. What I find confusing is trying to imagine that an ego, a personality, is actually reborn, in the sense that I might once have been Gustav Klimt, my neighbour, or Mother Mary.

If you adhere too strongly to such ideas, you will end up questioning your sanity. This line of reason is far from productive.

The Buddha said that, if you use dualistic thinking to try to understand what karma really is, who you were in the past, and who you will be in the future, then your head will explode in seven pieces. It is simply impossible. This is one of those questions that look after themselves, since they turn out to be irrelevant over time. Only if your ego is really big will you want to know what you were in the past and what you will be in the future.

Many years ago, my Vajrayana teacher appeared to me in the form of a vision, and soon afterwards I began to project all my dreams onto him. In retrospect, this vision was a very skilful means of stoking up my ego. I asked myself whether he might have recognized me, whether I was something special, and so on. I really struggled and had a great longing to somehow be someone special, someone important, doubtless because I had the feeling that I had never been special enough for my father. Add to this the whole cultural idea that a woman needs a man, and so on. At the time I really wanted to be something special to someone. Through the support of my teacher, this desire entered my consciousness with full force.

Today I think that this could be compared to the concept of transference from psychotherapy. It was a kind of drastic treatment. At the time I was a siladhara[15] and I held fast onto my training. That is what the rules are for, like the grab handles on a bus. When the bus drives off, you can hold tight and stand upright, without flying out of the window or falling over.

The rules are there to support your practice, but many people do not understand this. The point is not to hide behind the rules because you are afraid of life. The rules are there to provide orientation when you can no longer think clearly. When everything has calmed down again, you can simply let go – until the next storm comes. If I had had no supportive community in that situation, the things that were released in my mind might have got explosive. And now they are gone. This encounter with my teacher speeded up my healing process no end.

How do you explain the vision if you look back on it today? Do you now think it was caused by your teacher or your own mind?
I still do not know who did what. Knowing this was important to me once, but it is not an issue for me anymore. The unresolved matters with my father, my unfulfilled fantasies, the cultural concept of the strong man... all these mental constructs were totally inflamed by the vision. Now I understand that the whole situation was some kind of skilful means or medicine for me. That is why there are so many

teachers and so many approaches in Buddhism – so that a very wide range of needs can be met.

In Vajrayana Buddhism one often hears stories of teachers recognizing students.
Yes, this happens. I also think that my Vajrayana teacher recognized me. He never told me as much, since my ego would have made too much of it at the time. After all, I would not have been the only one he recognized; he probably recognizes hundreds of people. He is an advanced bodhisattva who has taken the appropriate vows and who takes responsibility for many people, not just little Santacitta.

The desire to be something special is quite familiar to me. The secret hope that I am already quite advanced, but I just don't know it myself – until a teacher comes along and recognizes me. What is this desire to be special all about?
I think everyone wants to be something special. The stronger the ego, the more you want to be special, either in an overt or in a covert way. There are many manifestations of this wanting to be special, but this desire will gradually shrink over time, through practice and also through therapy. If the ego is very wounded, then it must be healed through therapy to a certain extent before it can benefit from Buddhist practice, and then such issues simply fall away with time.

When people speak of rebirth in Buddhism, the expression 'karma' often comes up. Are the two closely connected?
Of course. The quality of a rebirth depends on karma. *Karma* means 'intentional action'. Your rebirth depends on your intentional actions – physical, verbal, and mental.

The quality of a rebirth does not necessarily relate to your material circumstances, such as whether you are rich or poor, but rather affects the extent to which your respective circumstances support your progress in the Dharma. In other words, whether there are many limiting factors or whether doors open for you, one after another.

In regard to my teachers, I have clearly had very good karma. There, all doors opened, whereas, in my ordinary life, all doors closed. This forced me in a certain direction that I would never have voluntarily chosen when I was twenty-eight.

I have also been lucky in my life with Buddhist teachers – take, for example, the mere fact that we met each other – and I have also met some very distinguished teachers in person. But I am unable to make as much out of it as you do.

You probably did not feel the same urgency as I did. But at the end of the day this does not matter – that is why it is important to trust your inner guidance. Everyone does what is right for them. It is not about how fast you are. The important thing is that you are moving in the right direction, and at a speed that is appropriate for you. Maybe you still have other things to attend to, and perhaps you had to meet your current husband first. You did what you did, and, at the same time, you are moving in the right direction.

Finding your own speed sounds reassuring. But one can develop something like spiritual ambition, can't one?

It is better to call it a sense of urgency. There is even a Pali word for it – *samvega*. The five contemplations or, in Vajrayana, the four thoughts that turn the mind to the Dharma, are there to awaken and kindle this *samvega*. This sense of urgency helps one to set wholesome priorities in life and to increasingly give up dependence on comfort of any kind.

A sense of urgency is helpful in any event, if we think about how vulnerable our bodies and minds are, and everything that can happen. I only need to think of the climate crisis. It is more than appropriate to think: let me not waste my life! This is not ambition, but a realistic perspective. I could die at any minute! In this life I have been born as a human being, but I do not know whether I will be born as a human again in the next life. When I lie on my deathbed, I might be afraid because I have not made sufficient effort; I might die with the feeling that I have not done my best.

I would like to return to the question of what I should believe as a Buddhist. Things that are described using spiritual or religious terms in Buddhism are seen as biochemical processes as far as science is concerned. When a person is dead, scientifically speaking there is nothing left. What is the mind? Can you explain this term?

There is consciousness – you can experience this yourself just like anyone else. However, the mind is one of those phenomena that modern science still cannot really explain. What is the mind? Who creates the mind? Is it the brain? One does not know, but you experience your mind in every moment and can observe it.

The ego, as I have already said, is the sum of thought patterns that have been built up over countless lives or at least over the course of this life. With progressive Buddhist practice, these patterns are increasingly thinned out until they are completely gone. Fully awakened people still have a character – they are not all the same – but there is no more attachment.

For the dualistic mind it is impossible to imagine how this really is. Someone who is fully awakened will continue to live with her body until it dies and returns to the elements. After her awakening she will continue to eat and drink, go to the doctor, and read the newspaper, but she no longer identifies herself with these affairs. There are just these two processes, the body and the mind, but there is nobody that they belong to: they are simply part of nature. There is no immutable core that is experienced as centre or as identity. The flame of wanting and doing is finally extinguished and, with that, complete awakening or nirvana is realized.

And how should I imagine what happens to someone who is fully awakened after the death of the body?
The Buddha did not want to speak about this. In Hinduism and other religions from this period, philosophizing was considered very important, but the Buddha taught that this was not really meaningful. In one of his sermons, he said: I know about the whole forest, but you only need to know about the few leaves in my hand in order to realize freedom from suffering.[16] He was referring to the four noble truths. If you truly understand them, that is enough for liberation.

You are not yet awakened, so how can you understand something like this, even if the Buddha explains it to you? You are – like me – still trapped in the dualistic mind. These things cannot be fully explained through language.

So, with Buddhist practice, I do not know at the beginning exactly what I am getting myself into. I can only see that there are people who have tried it, who seem to be doing well, and so I feel ready to give it a try.

That is it. It's as if you said, I have never been to Kathmandu, but I'm interested, and I want to go there now. The most important thing is that you set off in the right direction. You do not know what karma you have already accumulated. Sometimes huge breakthroughs can happen all of a sudden. But, if you hold on to them, you will guarantee they will not.

One understands this more and more clearly, the further along the path one is, and from ancient stories about the often absurd relationships between teachers and students. One understands this type of thing with the heart – this is not dualistic thinking but intuition.

How can one explain dualistic thinking?

Language is dualistic. For example, you only know what good means if you know what bad means. All words have an antonym – black and white, good and bad, large and small. I cannot say in absolute terms: I am small. Small in relation to what or whom? In relation to a particular woman, I am big, and in relation to another I am small.

Art – for example, poetry – can sometimes rise above such dualisms and transcend them. It communicates that which is between the lines, which cannot be grasped with words.

People who have attained higher levels of realization touch others similarly, and, if there is also a connection from a past life, then it is even stronger.

Do you think our dualistic language influences our whole view of the world?

Yes, thinking is shaped by language. We think in words. Nouns are the biggest problem here. They make us believe that something is really a separate thing, distinct from all other things, and this is deeply ingrained in us. If we were to talk about a clock not as 'a clock' but by saying, 'it clocks', using a verb, then this might come closer to the momentary, processual nature of reality. Language and concepts serve to reduce complexity so that we can live and communicate. Omitting the processual nature of phenomena from language is also a kind of simplification. Without it, our world might look quite different.

We have a body, so we must eat; we have to be part of society, so we must follow rules. Language is not a bad solution for the communication that all this requires. But it comes at the price of distorting our vision of reality. Through Buddhist practice we can counteract these distortions. This is the opportunity offered by human birth.

This is also why Buddhism is described as the middle way between two extremes: being concerned only with awakening and not everything that surrounds it, or being concerned only with everything that surrounds it and not with practice itself. Neither extreme offers a complete solution. We have to keep returning to the middle, and this simply takes as long as it takes.

Early Buddhism, the core teachings, originated in India more than 2,500 years ago. The Buddha gave a new interpretation to many expressions that were already in use at the time, for example, karma. He also introduced completely new concepts, for example, dependent origination and emptiness. At the time these two approaches went beyond the current thinking on liberation. The Buddha taught that true liberation can only take place through insight. He was concerned with the permanent liberation of the mind from greed, aversion, and delusion, not just with a temporary liberation that can be experienced through certain states of concentration. The stability of a calm and collected mind is the essential precondition for insight into dependent origination and emptiness – and this insight is the basis for actual liberation. This is wisdom.

When one begins to contemplate impermanence, unsatisfactoriness, and not-self or the emptiness of all things, these three characteristics of existence become Dharma doors, entrances to reality and through this to liberation. Other people also thought about impermanence at the time of the Buddha, for example the Greek scholar Heraclitus (around 520–460 BCE), who said one cannot step in the same river twice. The Buddha extrapolated from this and taught the emptiness of all phenomena. You cannot step in the River Danube, take something out, and say, this is the soul of the Danube. The whole river is called the Danube, and it is constantly changing. We simply call it Danube so that we can talk about it, but, in reality, the Danube is a process. The Danube has no unchanging core. This is the doctrine of emptiness.

One can say the same thing about gender. There is nothing that is essentially feminine or masculine. It seems that this notion is gradually moving into mainstream thinking – the recognition that there is no unchanging core at the heart of individual phenomena. However, when greed and aversion are triggered, when emotions become intense, we lose ourselves in the assumption of a separate existence, since our thinking is so profoundly shaped by the nouns in our language.

Because then the 'I' becomes very strong and, with it, fear.
That is why it is important, even in situations when one feels very challenged, to remind oneself that everything is a process, everything is transient, and that there is no permanence to things. Greed and aversion are gradually washed away through meditation, so that one no longer drowns when one is challenged. That is all you need to do – wash, wash, wash. Then you will see things more and more clearly; at the end you will not have gained anything, but you will have let go of a lot.

In our dualistic mindset it is hard to think of something positive in any other way than as something we get. But on the Buddhist path you give up more and more. At the end, all your wishes will have been fulfilled, simply because they will have dissolved to nothing. The washing takes place in stages, and sometimes our karma means that we need to go somewhere that looks like a detour. But it is not a detour.

One cannot work everything out on the meditation cushion. Some things require our complete involvement. If you cannot go around something, you need to go through it. Then it is better to go voluntarily and stop fooling yourself that you are further on than you really are. Do the thing that you so badly want to do, but at the same time ask yourself whether it is really that wonderful. At some point you will have had enough and it will be over. This is quicker than pretending to yourself, and that is why it is so important to be honest with yourself.

A Dent in the Patriarchy

Now I am coming to an important aspect of your Buddhist path, your womanhood. You were ordained as a bhikkhuni together with Ayya Anandabodhi in 2011. This highest level of ordination as a nun was denied to women in Theravada Buddhism for 1,000 years, until efforts began in the 1980s to reinstate it.[17] You contributed to this effort in a way that attracted international attention. Would you describe yourself as a feminist?

I am not sure exactly what you mean by feminist. I advocate for equal rights for women, and I do this not only for social but also for psychological reasons. It does something to our minds when we, as women, freely accept or are forced to adopt a subordinate position. If you really want to awaken and leave all delusions behind, then the whole of your mental capacity must be available, otherwise it is simply not possible.

Moreover, if you want to bring the qualities that lead to awakening fully into bloom, you will not manage it through meditation alone. You also need to create the right circumstances in your life, and must not allow yourself to be pushed aside. It is all part of the process. After all, realization means that our insight is integrated and lived. If you do not live your insights, they are not true insights.

When you decided to become a nun, one might say that a number of issues were resolved for you as a woman. Looking back now, what kind of a woman were you before you became a nun?

The thing that occurs to me first of all is that I was strongly influenced by my mother. She was very concerned with her appearance and very fashion-conscious. She had very narrow views about what beauty meant, and, in any event, she associated beauty with youth. Before I reached puberty, I was quite plump. My mother was unhappy about this, because she could not dress me as prettily as she would have liked to. Once she even told me this, which was very hurtful. When I became a teenager this all changed rapidly. When I joined the hotel-management school I turned from a girl into a young woman within a year. My mother had always wanted me to wear makeup, but initially I resisted this. I only started doing this later, when I went to Vienna to study.

At this time, in the early 1980s, I liked to dress in the style of the 1950s and as a punk. For a while I wore only black, powdered my face to make it white, and dyed my hair black and pink. Sometimes I wore men's suits with ties and everything. Clothes were very important to me at the time, and I had a great many, including beautiful old vintage dresses, mainly in black.

Were you happy with your appearance?
Of course not. When I look at old photos of myself today, I think I actually looked quite good. But that was not how it seemed to me at the time.

When you were young, did you dream of a husband, of children and a family?
Not really. I did want a husband, but I never gave much thought to starting a family. I had the feeling I had to go out into the world, to learn something and see other things. I was not happy in my romantic relationships. The unresolved issues with my father kept on manifesting with my partners. I felt attracted to men with whom I could only have unstable relationships. That was how I experienced the relationship with my father. I grew up in a hotel and never really knew when my parents would be available, when they would have time for me and when not. A hotel is an environment where strangers who are more important than the children are constantly appearing. Today one would describe this as unreliable emotional attachment. I instinctively found unreliable emotional attachment with men attractive, since I was familiar with it already.

The man whom I was together with for ten years had a very dominating mother. He played out his issues with me, and I played out mine with him. We looked for each other and found each other. In a sense we were made for each other, because each reflected what the other had known in their childhood.

All of this happened at a time when political feminism was becoming more powerful in universities. What was your stance towards this?
I admit I was interested in it, but at the same time it was also important to me to look chic, and at the time this was not appropriate for a feminist. Somehow, I stood between the two camps. I had no idea at all who I was or what I wanted.

On my first journey to Asia, I was deeply saddened to see how people there strived to become entangled in the same consumer society as the one I came from. At the time I began to understand that coming to grips with greed, aversion, and delusion at a political level by, for example, donating to charity or supporting development projects is a superficial and extremely limited approach. The root of the problem goes much deeper – it is essential to cultivate the mind. I grasped this quite quickly at an intuitive level, but I did not know that this is exactly where a religion like Buddhism begins.

When I saw the monks on the train in Myanmar in 1987, I knew: this is it. One year later, in 1988, I met Ajahn Buddhadasa, and it was clear to me that this was how I wanted to be. I did not necessarily imagine my life as a nun, but I wanted to develop this way of being for myself. Initially I just wanted to stay at the monastery for a time and then finish my studies. It would have really interested me to work as an art anthropologist, particularly in the area of ritual, dance, and theatre. Time passed, and then the university gave me a deadline of 2003 for the submission of my half-finished thesis. I knew that I would lose everything if I did not finish writing it.

However, at that point I did not feel stable enough to leave the monastery to live in Vienna again and resume my academic work. In the end I decided to leave my doctorate unfinished. Completing it would have meant setting my robe aside, since my dissertation about dance and theatre was not really compatible with my monastic training. I also did not want to start again with another topic, for example, life in a Buddhist monastery in Asia. I threw all my academic material away, a whole laundry basket full of paper.

Why did you choose to become a nun? You could also have had a serious practice as a layperson and still had a romantic relationship.
At the monastery I saw many nuns come and go; they stayed two, five, or ten years. I thought that I was one of them, and that one day the door would open for me again. But I did not want to leave just because I wanted to have a partner, without any other plans. I did actually fall in love twice in the monastery, but it never turned into a relationship. That was simply not the path I was meant to take.

You have always led a very independent life and done what you wanted. Have you ever had the feeling that women were suppressed in general, or disadvantaged in practical terms?
I must say that before entering the monastery this was never really a major issue for me. I never felt oppressed personally, since I actually had a lot of freedom. In the monastery it was different. This was also the reason why in 1995, after two years as anagarika,[18] I temporarily left Amaravati[19] again. It was too patriarchal for me there. I travelled around, spending time in Thailand and the United States, looking for a place to train as a nun that was not as dominated by men.

What gave you the impression that Amaravati was patriarchal?
Everything. In daily things like queuing for the food counter. The monks, the bhikkhus, always went first in everything. More than anything it was evident from the fact that it was not possible for women to become ordained as bhikkhunis, as fully ordained nuns. It was clear that, in this system, the monks would always have the upper hand. We could become siladharas, which is a hybrid nuns' ordination created by the Ajahn Chah tradition in the West, to which Amaravati and

Chithurst monasteries belong. Originally this was thought to serve as a kind of intermediate solution, since then it was still generally assumed that the higher ordination for women in the Theravada had been irretrievably lost. In retrospect, the siladhara ordination was, at the time of its establishment in 1983, a truly innovative experiment, which was recognized internationally until around 2007 as an excellent training for nuns. However, after the revival of the Theravada bhikkhuni tradition was put beyond dispute, this intermediate solution lost its original function and became a kind of cul-de-sac, and was therefore obsolete.

When did it become obvious to you that you could not stay at Amaravati?
When I became more senior and got involved in more and more committees and steering groups. There it became increasingly evident that men had the control and would not even pass on certain pieces of information. It also became clear to me that things would continue in this way for a very, very long time. This all strengthened my resolve to leave.

In 2007 His Holiness the Dalai Lama called an international conference on bhikkhuni ordination in Hamburg, Germany. At the time, many monks, nuns, and laypeople came together from both camps: those who had demonstrated quite clearly that bhikkhuni ordination could be revived, and their opponents, who did not want to hear of it. The monks from the Ajahn Chah tradition were among the opponents, and so it was clear to me that I could no longer support this system.

Can you explain briefly the arguments used by opponents of the revival of bhikkhuni ordination?

It was argued that bhikkhuni ordination had died out in the Theravada sangha. It was passed on exclusively in the Mahayana until 1988 and in the Vajrayana it might never have really existed, although this has not yet been clarified.

The female tradition in the Theravada was, until recently, considered to have been interrupted for more than 1,000 years, and it was assumed that monks alone could not revive bhikkhuni ordination because for this one would need monks *and* nuns. In addition, it was assumed that a Theravada ordination with the support of Mahayana nuns was not possible. That was the opinion of certain monks, while others – learned Theravada monks – proved that the Buddha would definitely have allowed the revival of the bhikkhuni tradition, even if there were no nuns, or until there were enough nuns to make it possible.

Bhikkhu Bodhi, Bhikkhu Anālayo, Ajahn Brahm, and other internationally renowned monks demonstrated in a simple and comprehensible way that it was not an insurmountable problem. In Buddhism there is no spiritual head, like a pope, who could have decided this issue decisively one way or another.

The situation escalated in summer 2009. In the middle of this international discussion about bhikkhuni ordination, the monks from the Ajahn Chah tradition issued the so-called five points for the siladhara nuns. These five points set in stone the fact that higher ordination as bhikkhunis was not permitted to nuns of our tradition.

If you ask me, the issue was about power and the fear of having to share decision-making and resources, like in any other organization; and then there was an attempt to find a theological underpinning for the opposition.

How did your fellow sisters at Amaravati speak about this topic?
Our female community was divided. There was a wide range of nuns – young, old, Asian, European, American, Australian; they spoke different languages and came from different social and cultural backgrounds. Some said, we do not need this, we can become enlightened even without being ordained as bhikkhunis.

Others – and I was one of them – said, it has an effect on your mind if you are always of secondary importance to the monks. This is not a side issue. It affects you if you support a system that discriminates against women, and I did not want to do this to myself any longer. If your mind is not really brave, how will it awaken?

The nuns were not able to reach common ground on such an important issue, and so we agreed that each of us had to make her own decision. Of the siladharas in Amaravati and Chithurst, about half disrobed and a couple kept their robes but left. The other half remained at Amaravati. They were prepared to reconcile themselves to the situation.

Was it an easy decision for you to leave?
For me the decision was not hard because I could do nothing else. Of course, it was risky and frightening for me. I was over fifty at the time, and had been a member of the monastic community for nearly two decades. But I felt very clearly that this was what I had to do.

We were invited by the Saranaloka Foundation in the United States to set up a branch of Amaravati there. This foundation was established in 2005, with the objective of supporting the siladharas of the Ajahn Chah tradition, so that they could become more independent of the monks. In the first instance it was about providing material support. The foundation invited the siladharas from Amaravati and Chithurst to the United States to teach or go on retreat there. And, as a second step, the siladharas were to go to the United States to establish a training monastery there.

In 2007, before the so-called five points were issued, a letter from Jill Boone, the founding president of the Saranaloka Foundation, arrived. She wrote that there was a promising plot of land that one of the siladharas ought to come and look at. We somehow managed to arrange things so that Ayya Anandabodhi and I were allowed to travel to the United States for six weeks and look at this property. We had to pass up on our winter retreat to make it possible. And that was how it all began. We travelled around the US and visited Oregon, Washington, Oklahoma, and California in search of fertile ground. At some point it became clear to us that it would be San Francisco, and that we wanted to come back. The Saranaloka Foundation rented a house for our return, initially for two months and then from the end of 2009 on a long-term basis. At the same time, we knew that we wanted to leave the city at some point, since we are from the Forest Tradition.

In the United States at this time there were already some bhikkhunis. After we had arrived, Ayya Anandabodhi and I soon understood that we did not want to compete with these bhikkhunis with our homemade siladhara model; they lived the way the Buddha himself had recommended a long time ago. In many of his teachings he spoke about the fourfold sangha made up of bhikkhus, bhikkhunis, lay men, and lay women.

As soon as we realized that we wanted to take bhikkhuni ordination, we arranged a telephone call with Ajahn Sumedho and Ajahn Amaro, the abbot and the deputy abbot at Amaravati. In this conversation we explained that we wanted to become bhikkhunis. Naturally, neither of the abbots wanted anyone else to leave after so many siladharas had already left Amaravati. The Amaravati senior monastics would have allowed us to establish a branch in the United States, but it was clear at that point that we could not really act as representatives for the Ajahn Chah lineage in California.

We therefore decided to leave the lineage in order to become bhikkhunis. A representative of the monks explained to us that the monastery leadership was about to permit bhikkhuni ordination for siladharas very shortly, and that this process would only be delayed by our departure. However, we did not believe this and were right not to, since there is still no bhikkhuni ordination at Amaravati.

Where did support for your bhikkhuni ordination come from?
Mainly from the Saranaloka Foundation, of course. When we decided that we would become bhikkhunis and leave the Ajahn Chah lineage, we did not ask the Saranaloka Foundation in advance whether they would support us. We wanted to leave it up to the foundation to decide whether they would continue to support us or not. Half of the board members wanted to have nothing to do with our leaving the tradition,

and they quit the foundation. Three of them remained and continued to support us.

Help also came from other organizations, in particular from Spirit Rock. Jack Kornfield, one of the founders of this large retreat centre in California, had been a monk in the Ajahn Chah tradition. Many other more open-minded Buddhist teachers rallied around him. Things went very well. Then there was also help from the Insight Meditation Society – IMS – from Joseph Goldstein and Sharon Salzberg. This is the counterpart to Spirit Rock on the East Coast of the United States.

IMS and Spirit Rock are the largest retreat centres of the Theravada Insight Tradition in the United States. If one receives support from them, then of course this is excellent: we were in the right place at the right time. Ajahn Chah monks had taught in these centres for many years and sometimes also brought nuns with them. Many people noticed that the nuns always walked behind the monks, and this led to disapproval.

At the time, Ruth Denison (1922–2015), a famous, rather eccentric teacher, was also teaching at Spirit Rock. Born in Germany, she was a pioneer of Buddhism in the West and a trailblazer for women's rights. This influential teacher had provided the original impetus for the establishment of the Saranaloka Foundation.

How did things progress for you in the United States?
From the end of 2009 we settled in the United States, and after nine months, in autumn 2010, we made it public that we would be leaving the Ajahn Chah tradition. We planned to travel to Amaravati in April 2011, in order to bid a formal

farewell to the community there. Our bhikkhuni ordination was to take place in October 2011.

We left plenty of time between the various steps, so that things could calm down in between. After leaving the siladhara training, we travelled back to the United States and, a couple of days later, we were ordained as samaneris, or novices.

Ayya Tathaloka, a fully ordained American senior nun, made our ordination possible. The bhikkhuni ordination took place on 17 October 2011 at Spirit Rock. Jack Kornfield and the executive director of Spirit Rock acted as masters of ceremonies, and monks and nuns from all three schools of Buddhism were present. Looking back, this was quite an unusual situation, since it brought together supporters from many orientations. Bhikkhuni ordination became more or less mainstream on that day.

In 2014 we actually left San Francisco for the countryside. For a number of years, the forest fires in this area have been increasingly devastating and, in the meantime, we have decided to leave this place again. Perhaps forest monasteries in California are a thing of the past, since they take too much effort to maintain in the face of climate change. We will have to think of something else and adapt to the times; that is just how it is – after all, we are samanas, which, in Pali, means 'homeless ones'.

So in 2011 you and Ayya Anandabodhi were finally able to receive bhikkhuni ordination. What does this require?
At the material level it requires a robe and an alms bowl. For the ceremony itself, a bhikkhuni who has been ordained for

at least twelve years and a further five bhikkhus and five bhikkhunis must be present. At the ceremony the presiding nun declares in public that the woman in question is ready to become a bhikkhuni. The whole process with all its detail takes less than an hour. Normally a woman has to spend at least five years in a monastery before she can become an independent bhikkhuni. You must spend at least one of these years living in white as an anagarika on eight precepts, and then two years as a samaneri, on ten precepts. Then two years as a bhikkhuni with a bhikkhuni teacher who instructs you. After that you can travel and stay at other monasteries if you want to.

Bhikkhus need to spend five years with their teacher, bhikkhunis only two. There is no official reason for this; it is one of the few areas where things are easier for nuns than for monks.

Has the turmoil around your departure from the Ajahn Chah tradition subsided in the meantime?
Naturally there was initially tension after we left Amaravati. I think Ayya Anandabodhi and I have probably gone down as revolutionaries in the history of the Ajahn Chah tradition. But things have calmed down over the years. Today I feel huge gratitude for the support I received from the Ajahn Chah sangha in England and Thailand. Without this training, Ayya Anandabodhi and I would never have had the strength, the skill, and the connections necessary to establish our own monastery, built completely on donations, within the existing Buddhist system.

In 1992, when I left Thailand for Amaravati, Amaravati and Chithurst in England were the only monasteries in the

West offering proper training for women. From a material perspective it was an unbelievably generous situation, but unfortunately the conditions for women got more constrictive over time.

When I started my anagarika training in 1993, everything seemed wide open and many things seemed possible. From around 2007, however, the situation began to change. The training in these monasteries is still very good, but with the proviso that women are only accorded permanent novice status.

As a nun you may not feel surprised by much. But has there been anything between the time when you entered that first monastery and the present day that has surprised you?
What surprised me was the behaviour of the men at Amaravati and Chithurst. After all, some of them are teachers who are deeply respected worldwide. Many women come and help with the running of the monastery. They said quite openly: we need the nuns, but only if they stay in their place.

For me, leaving was not a difficult decision. I could also simply have disrobed, but I did not want to do that. As a Buddhist nun who is not part of a tradition dominated by conservative men, I have a lot of creative leeway and can therefore reach people who feel that their needs are not met by traditional Buddhism. It is not about changing the teachings, but about imparting them in a way that is appropriate to the times.

I am not in the least interested in maintaining a general antagonism with the men. When women use the capacities and opportunities that are available to them to the utmost, then of course this helps men too. Life on this planet is becoming increasingly precarious. I am not interested in power, but rather in using all of our potential, so that half of humanity on this planet is not excluded from participation. That would be a meaningless waste of potential!

With the work that Ayya Anandabodhi and I have done in recent years, we have made a sizeable dent in the wall of the patriarchy.

In doing so, you have done something for all women in Buddhism, not just yourselves.
Absolutely. We were not just two women who popped up and wanted to become bhikkhunis: we always had the restitution of the bhikkhuni sangha in mind. It goes without saying that we were afraid of being criticized, since our approach was quite bold, but it was not our intention to cast the Ajahn Chah lineage in a bad light. At the same time, we wanted to use the chance to do what we felt was right; we managed to cause a stir without meaning to, and attract quite a bit of attention.

What concrete things are you doing for women now?
More than anything we are examples, role models for women. We turn up at a Buddhist centre and enjoy trust and respect as teachers. You don't see that very often. Guests can visit us and live with us for a while, on the basis of voluntary donations. You have to help out with the work, but everyone can afford it. This is a great gift in this day and age. We also offer spiritual guidance, and women who are suitable can train with us to become nuns themselves. The only condition for this is that they join in and are able to become part of the community.

Is there anything specifically feminine in the way that you teach Buddhism?
I cannot really generalize about that. I am very interested in the climate movement and in bringing it together with the Buddha's teachings. Instead of speaking theoretically about the feminist cause, I try to live it. That suits me better. We were brave enough to step away from a powerful lineage and do our own thing. Some people have asked themselves whether hell will swallow us up, because we abandoned our teacher.

But I would not actually say that I broke off with my teacher. I still cherish and respect him as I always have, but I have broken away from accepting the teaching in those aspects that no longer correspond to our time. I am certain that this does no harm to the teaching. The bhikkhuni form already existed 2,500 years ago – we did not invent it. The bhikkhu and the bhikkhuni lineages have probably both been interrupted from time to time. Only the bhikkhu lineage was revived again without too much fuss, while with the bhikkhuni lineage nothing happened; it was as if people were waiting for a time when they could finally get rid of it.

In your experience, do men and women practise differently?
No, there are no substantial differences between men and women. One could perhaps define certain feminine and masculine traits though, and I could make some general observations about those. For example, in a group of nuns, everyone will know about everyone else, to an extent that can be almost intrusive. A monk, by contrast, might not even know if the monk in the next room is considering suicide. Men generally have less capacity for relationships and women

sometimes have too much. That is a tendency that women can have when they live together. At least that is my experience from monastery life. I find it helpful to have already accumulated quite a lot of experience in a large international community like Amaravati: it means I know what I need to look out for, and that is very helpful.

The Power to Say No

You once mentioned that you have reconsidered your decision to become a nun several times and decided in favour of it again and again.

Sometimes I get asked why I live a life of renunciation. It seems fitting to compare the situation with that of a top athlete. She has a regulated diet, trains for many hours per day, avoids doing certain things and instead does others regularly. Instead of training muscles, I am training my mind. This is completely voluntary, but some people who are not interested in this kind of sport might consider it extreme. They think that someone who does this must be crazy.

You use the word 'renunciation' in this context, and that is really not very sexy.

Yes, not sexy at all, actually. I am also trying to think of another word for it, since I know that for many people it provokes rejection. But the expression is fitting. Renunciation is one of the ten perfections in Theravada Buddhism. In contemporary language I would call it energy saving. We all have only a certain amount of energy available, and it is our decision to use it in one way and not in another.

In discussions about measures to tackle the climate crisis it is also unattractive to talk about relinquishment.
Nobody likes renunciation or relinquishment. In our patriarchal, neoliberal consumer culture, relinquishment is always seen as loss. However, you could also say that being able to say no is a powerful capacity. Someone with a weak mind or a weak character cannot do this. Afraid of being left out if they do not do the same as everyone else, they cannot imagine swimming against the current. It is hard to score points by telling people, 'Being able to say no is a good thing, you need to learn this, it is empowering.' Saying no is hard to sell and has a bad reputation in our society. It just goes to show how much we are annihilating ourselves through capitalism and through our unchecked consumerist behaviour. Being able to say no has become a question of survival on this planet.

However, one should be very clear about one's own motivation for relinquishment. It can spoil the whole situation if one judges others who do not want to or are not able to relinquish or renounce.

How far does renunciation need to go? Total asceticism was surely not what the Buddha had in mind, was it?
The Buddha left his family, shaved his head, and practised strict asceticism for the first few years. The canon says that at times he only ate three grains of rice per day. He was so emaciated that, when he touched his back, he could feel his breastbone. His practice was not successful then, since he was so weakened that he could no longer meditate.

There is a famous story about a young girl who was taking rice pudding to a shrine in the forest as an offering. On the way she saw the Buddha sitting under a tree and gave the rice pudding to him. The Buddha ate it and felt revived, and then his practice could continue.

After that he remembered sitting under a rose-apple tree as a child while his father carried out the ceremony of the first spring ploughing. At the time he experienced a very peaceful and joyful meditation. He remembered that he did not need to be afraid of this kind of joy, since this kind of subtle joy supports the practice by expanding and energizing the mind. He clearly understood that practice needs a certain amount of joy. If there is no joy in the mind, it will simply not open. However, this is not the kind of joy that is experienced through the senses, and to which one often becomes attached. This other kind of joy is the result of an independence from things, of letting go. This is a different kind of joy from what is felt when one gets what one wants. In Buddhist texts it is therefore described as unworldly joy. It arises in the mind when the mind is really in the present moment and not attached.

How does one begin to feel this subtle joy? Is it when one starts to meditate?
One has to learn to recognize this subtle joy, because it is easily overlooked. Beginners in Buddhist practice can often sense it very easily. This is beginner's luck, but, when they start to become attached to it, it becomes difficult.

How up-to-date is Buddhism? Does Western society today need Buddhism?
I would not say that the world needs Buddhism. The world needs spiritual systems that people can use, and Buddhism is one of them. The important thing is that people have

instructions to help them overcome the deep conditioning we are all caught up in – for example, believing that we need to take as much from nature as we possibly can. We do not understand that we are part of nature, part of the planet.

The planet is a closed system that we cannot escape from, as long as we exist as humans. Whatever we put into this system will at some point come back to us. Understanding that is the task – what takes place in the classroom, if you like – when one is born as a human being.

If I think about my own life, I can see that I live in relative security, I can afford to heat my apartment, and I have a small but regular income. Actually, I have a very comfortable life. Why should I turn to a spiritual system like Buddhism?

We have comfortable lives now, but we do not know how long things will carry on like this. It is not guaranteed that everything will continue so smoothly until your death or mine. The ecological system is incredibly fragile and could be brought to a tipping point at any time. In the last few years many things have happened that we could not have imagined before.

Do you mean phenomena connected to climate change or social developments?

It's all connected, isn't it? The effects of the climate crisis will increase and intensify all of the other tensions and conflicts. Having said that, I do not believe that, as humans, we have done anything fundamentally wrong. We learn and we experiment; that is evolution. In the last 150 years we have taken many short-sighted decisions, mainly in connection with the increasing exploitation of fossil fuels. We used this apparently cheap source of energy unwisely, since we genuinely believed that it was cheap. For the longest time, it looked to humanity as if the developments that are now unbalancing the planet had no price.

Now we are becoming increasingly aware that our immature lifestyle has a very high price, and this is a great opportunity to awaken. Before the Industrial Revolution many people lived in relative harmony with nature and the planet, and we can find our way back to this state. More and more people will need to recognize the interdependence between the human and the more-than-human world. This interdependence is based on a Buddhist core principle, the principle of emptiness.

Emptiness means that nothing originates, exists, or disappears just by itself. Everything is connected to everything else. Take, for example, the water here in my glass. We do not know where it really comes from. Is it the rain, the ocean, the lakes, or the rivers? In a closed system it is always the same water. This includes the water in our bodies, which we let go of when we go to the toilet or cry.

The principle of emptiness is very central to all schools of Buddhism. The Venerable Thich Nhat Hanh (1926–2022) coined the word 'interbeing' to express this, which I find extremely fitting. Indigenous cultures and systems theory are based on the appreciation of these interrelationships of life, and we must learn to respect this kind of wisdom if we want to restructure our way of life in sustainable ways. It is assumed that, today, 80 per cent of the biodiversity on Earth can be found on indigenous lands.

Which Buddhist concepts can be helpful with respect to the climate crisis?

In times like this, I would like to spend more time speaking about the principle of dependent origination and to pass on this wisdom. For this, one does not necessarily need to put the focus on Buddhism. Getting involved with an Asian religion may be too much for most people, but, if one is looking for some kind of spiritual training, and if it really works, then a curiosity to go deeper and get to the roots of that training will automatically arise.

When life gets hard, one needs inspiration. Religious symbols and forms are skilful means for awakening inspiration. The concept of being part of a tradition of practitioners that is more than 2,500 years old can give one strength. But one does not need to go all the way immediately: the Buddha's teachings can be added later, if desired.

Does anything need to be added at all?

Through my many years of experience I can say that a serious practice through which one experiences really deep transformation will not take place without some sort of support or connection, but this does not have to be Buddhism.

If you look at your deep conditioning, you are bound to experience suffering or dissonance for at least some of the time. The Buddha therefore also said that spiritual friends are the most important element on the Buddhist path.

There are different approaches to deconditioning or reconditioning the mind through practice and meditation. Our whole culture is based on the idea that having more means being more secure, and we are now seeing that this is not at all true. It's about letting go, not accumulating even more! For me this is the gist of Buddhism and also of the whole situation on our planet. The point is not to learn something new that you do not already know. The point is to let go, through insight, of emotional and cognitive filters that cloud perception and, in so doing, to gradually see more clearly.

We need to change our behaviour significantly and learn to understand what science has known for a long time: that we are a part of the planet, and that we are made up of identical elements to the planet itself. Integrating this insight into our lives is the next evolutionary step in the development of human consciousness on this planet. We are not a separate species, wandering around on the planet as if on a stage. We are the planet itself.

In history there have been drastic changes in awareness of this magnitude from time to time, and they have often been accompanied by chaos and bloodshed. For example, in the course of the French Revolution people suddenly became aware that it was not God who determined who was king and queen, whose sumptuous lifestyle they had to support even though they were poor. It was all wrong! The king and queen were ordinary people just like them. At the moment we are in a similar situation: more and more people are starting to understand that planet Earth does not belong to us, so we cannot simply take what we want, regardless of the consequences. Recognizing that, by doing so, we are actually injuring ourselves takes us to a higher or broader level of consciousness. Such a shift in consciousness is difficult without spiritual practice, if not impossible. You cannot knock a hole in your head with a hammer and chisel, to encourage your mind to expand – you have to know how it works. But Buddhism is certainly not the only method available.

However, most systems of spiritual practice currently still have a very patriarchal character. The basic problem with a patriarchal orientation is that it makes relationships based on equality impossible. Patriarchal structures in combination with the powerful technologies that we have today can lead to very dangerous situations.

What we need now is diversity and multiplicity, varied and different kinds of knowledge. Everyone has something to contribute, all gender identities, indigenous nations, and more-than-human beings such as rivers, trees, and mountains. We need to take this developmental step together.

Speaking of powerful technologies: the effects of meditation on the brain can be demonstrated. Could this change in consciousness be created artificially, like recording a hard drive, for example?
Not at all. We still do not know what the mind is. The mind is not just located in the brain, and consciousness exists throughout the whole body. We can say that the body is actually in the mind. You sense that you are sitting here, and all around you there is limitless space. If I listen into the stillness, my mind becomes wide open, and my body is in my mind – not the other way around. There are states where the mind, consciousness, or awareness – you can also call it that – is completely wide open.

While we are talking to each other, you can be aware of your body, how it is sitting here; you can see me and the table, you can hear the clock ticking and be aware of the voices outside in the street. At the same time, you also know that the sun, the moon, and the stars are up there, above us. You can know all of this with your mind. And it is not your mind – it is simply mind, as such.

The first of the three refuges of Buddhism implies merely resting in awareness. This awareness is also referred to as 'buddha'. The best way to think of it is like a mirror that effortlessly reflects everything that passes before it.

Buddhist practice is about consciously dwelling in awareness instead of focusing on that which we want either more or less of. We are instructed to become aware of the pressures and urges of greed and aversion, without reacting to them immediately. If something gives us a pleasant feeling, we attempt to hold on to it. That is, we begin to interfere with the river of life. And we often start this process from a very egocentric standpoint, as the climate crisis clearly illustrates.

There are a couple of concepts here that I am finding hard to reconcile. There are these huge problems – for example, the climate crisis – where we are all called upon to change our behaviour. How does this fit together with the imperative, or the advice, not to intervene?

The most important thing about non-interference is to see how much we interfere in everything, all the time: to recognize what effects this interference has. Sometimes one simply has to interfere, in order to limit some greater interference – for example, by standing up against the destruction of the biosphere. Non-interference does not mean indifference. I get involved in climate activism whenever I can. The key is to interfere as little as possible from the standpoint of greed, aversion, or delusion.

Are you pessimistic or optimistic about our ability to manage the climate crisis?
I think we can still change course. There are already countless people and organizations who understand this. There are many feedback loops that we can no longer stop, and there will be more natural disasters. There have always been and always will be chaos and pain involved in major change. You can compare it to a birth: chaos is the precursor to a new order – this is how evolution works and how development happens.

Processes like these are not a walk in the park, and this is why it is important to have a practice so that one does not lose oneself in fear and can maintain a certain degree of balance. If one has not cultivated the seven factors of awakening, it is hard to maintain the right perspective, and then one will lack the mental and emotional strength to see the long-term benefit within such processes.

So you are assuming there will be an evolution of consciousness? That there is an emerging awareness that humans are part of something much greater and not creation's crowning achievement?
The Christian injunction to subdue the Earth is one of the core principles of patriarchy. It is how, in combination with technological progress and the exploitation of fossil fuels, the current climate crisis came about. Worldviews function for a certain period of time and then need to be replaced by something else – that is evolution. Spiritual practice helps to oil the wheels and make this process less painful, since one learns that everything is in a constant state of flux and that attachment therefore leads to suffering. If something old no longer works, it falls apart. In the autumn, the leaves fall to

the ground, rot, and turn into nutrition for the tree, and, in the spring, there are new ones.

Through spiritual practice you will acquire a general overview of what it means to be born human. With a spiritual practice you will have much less fear, because you will have some kind of roadmap and know a couple of more experienced travellers who can reassure you that you are on the right track.

If you were to assume that not a single person on this planet was spiritual, would this shift in consciousness still take place? Is consciousness moving in this direction in any event?

The assumption would be meaningless, since there are spiritual people. I can see that a development in consciousness is happening, even if I do not know where it is going. For about 4.5 billion years, since the planet began to take shape, a development towards greater complexity has doubtless been taking place. From a given stage, reflexive consciousness developed, which distinguishes our species *Homo sapiens* from others. As a result, for example, we are able to cooperate in large groups. But then our species became so powerful that it displaced all other species in the genus *Homo* who could not do this at all or as well.

It could be that Homo sapiens *will one day destroy its habitat and die out. Would consciousness or awareness continue to exist on Earth? What would happen to this river of consciousness that we have put so much effort into through our Buddhist practice?*

It is not just the Earth, but the whole cosmos that is aware. In simple terms, we are an immature species that is out of control. Many species have already died out who could not or would not participate in the way they needed to in order to survive.

And it is not *our* river of consciousness – it is simply awareness per se. It belongs to no one. Another species of human will probably develop on the basis of our achievements, just as we stand on the shoulders of our predecessors. In Early Buddhism one speaks of cycles that repeat themselves again and again. Perhaps there will be a species of *Homo* that will have the edge over us because they live in the understanding that they are part of this planet, a '*Homo ecologiensis*'.

Awareness itself, what is called *dharmakaya* in Vajrayana or *buddho* in the Thai Forest Tradition, cannot be lost. It has no beginning and no end. There are many names for it. In the Christian faith, for example, it is called God; in Islam, Allah, and, in indigenous cultures, Great Spirit.

I have no doubt that everything that exists is a form of intelligence that we cannot really understand or grasp intellectually. But we can cultivate the seven factors of awakening and, in so doing, dissolve all the filters that are between us and that which one cannot really name. One can experience this in moments when the mind is free from all desires and simply rests in awareness.

Is that a moment of enlightenment?
I prefer to say awakening. In this moment one sees things as they really are. This is a foretaste of nirvana, the unconditioned, and a freedom from desire, a moment of clear seeing, when our experience is not distorted by our own hopes and fears. As we practise meditation, our capacity for conscious resting in awareness gets stronger, and the time we can spend in that state is extended.

This kind of connectedness, a sense of being part of something greater than oneself, is experienced as enrichment or safety that cannot be bought with money. When one truly understands this, the whole world of consumption seems like a nuisance; one finds joy in small things and enjoys spending time in nature. Spiritual practice should be a part of any education. Just as we learn to write and to calculate, we should learn how to communicate with the larger context of existence.

Nature is not centrally controlled. No one can dominate or control nature. The important thing is discovering how we can accept our humble place in the larger scheme of things and be content with it. The important thing is recognizing interdependence and seeing that, as long as we exist in any form, we can never escape from these complex and messy relationships, because we have not yet realized full awakening.

And what are the prospects for someone who is still far away from such insights? How can they cope with the uncertainties caused by the climate crisis?

We are used to constantly striving to protect ourselves. However, this does not really work, because something unexpected always happens. The Covid pandemic is a good example. True security can only be achieved if we make ourselves completely vulnerable. Paradoxically, when one recognizes vulnerability completely, one becomes invulnerable.

Wanting nothing, in the sense that you no longer have any irrevocable ideas as to how things have to be, is the best precaution you can take. But this is diametrically opposed to our habitual ways of thinking. If you really want to open yourself to creativity, you need to have the courage also to open yourself to ignorance, despair, fear, or shame and to trust that new answers will come to you. In the English-speaking world people talk a great deal about 'emergence' these days – about the arrival of new solutions, new approaches, through which the inherent intelligence of life itself speaks to us in a certain way. For this we must have the courage to open ourselves to the situation, such as it really is.

Buddhism does not give us any answers, but it gives us the tools to open ourselves fully to our own experience. If we can face up to this challenge of not knowing what to do, we will be able to recognize where our contribution lies.

This 'emergence' is a spiritual principle. New kinds of understanding will come to the fore and, with them, new answers. We are part of a global civilization and have created this situation together, and so we have to solve it together, too. We must all do our best to open ourselves to these new stimuli. Those who have trained their minds and let go of at least some of the filters will be better placed than those who prefer not to look, for fear of what they might see. The most important thing of all is to do the right thing, that is, to act in harmony with your own insights and your own values. There are more than enough things that need doing in this world. One person might feel themselves drawn to Black Lives Matter, another to the climate movement; yet another to working as a doctor or a journalist in a war zone. And some to becoming a nun or a monk.

How does such engagement fit in with the idea of letting go?
This is a paradox. You do what you can to fix the world, and, at the same time, you know that it cannot really be fixed.

Samsara cannot be repaired. Samsara is not a place; it is a state of mind. You can only repair samsara in your own mind, by developing more and more capacity to open yourself up to your own experience with equanimity. Through this, the answers will also become clear, and you will realize your insights by living them. The word 'realize' means 'to bring into existence, make, or cause to become real', and here this means incorporating what you have recognized in your meditation into your own conduct.

This gives you a sense of enrichment and meaning. This meaning does not lie in the fact that the world will one day be perfect. That will never be the case, but the ideal functions as a guiding light. On the path, the mind will become more and more free of cognitive and emotional filters. The more greed, aversion, and delusion are washed away from the mind, the more space one has around one's own experiences and the less one is identified with them. This is the proverbial hut in the snowstorm.

The insights you gain through meditation are only true insights if you integrate them into your life and organize your life accordingly. For example, if you really see the suffering of animals, at some point you can simply no longer eat meat.

You once organized a meditation weekend with the title, 'Learning from Nature'. What did you mean by this?
As I have said already, one can translate the word 'Dharma' in many different ways. 'Dharma' means, among other things, 'nature' or 'the laws of nature'. This is why there are forest monasteries: because the forest illustrates impermanence so well, for example, when old trees fall down and rot in the

ground, and new trees grow in their place. In the forest it is easy to understand the cycle of life. It brings us back to the truly fundamental processes: to impermanence and to the insight that everything comes into being interdependently.

The rose in your garden originated in reliance on the soil, the rain, the sun, the seed, the house that it can climb up, and so on. The rose by itself does not exist, it is a coming together of all the things I have just listed. If you cut the rose from the bush and divide it into 500,000 parts, you will not be able to show me a single part that is the rose. The rose in and of itself does not exist; neither do you or I. This is emptiness.

Emotions and Mindfulness

In Buddhism people often talk about training the mind. You have compared yourself to a top athlete, and I can imagine what a marathon runner does when she trains, but what does training the mind involve? What is actually being trained here?

Certain capacities or mental qualities, described as the seven awakening factors (*bojjhanga*), are trained. I will list them again here: mindfulness, investigation, energy, joy, tranquillity, stability, and equipoise. Everyone is born with these qualities, at least at a rudimentary level, in their own mind, since they are needed for every skill one needs to learn.

I want to return to the expression 'training'. For ordinary practitioners, what does progress look like? What increases and decreases in the course of one's training?

This is identical for all practitioners, whether they are ordained or not. As I have already mentioned several times, the cognitive and emotional filters through which we see reality become thinner and fewer. They are thinned out and dissolved through practice until they have completely disappeared. When these filters are no longer there, one can see things as they really are. One can see more clearly, influenced less and less by one's own desires, hopes, and fears.

Someone who sees reality incorrectly will not be aware that they are doing so. How will I know when I am seeing things in the correct way?

When the mind is free from wanting and not-wanting, when the mind is simply open and unattached, then one sees things as they are for us, from our perspective as *Homo sapiens*. Wanting and not-wanting distort the view. A simple example: assume you are walking down a street and you are very hungry. Normally you would not notice how many restaurants there are in this street, but, because you are so hungry, you see restaurants everywhere; you see the street in a different light from usual, and the restaurants practically jump out at you. This is not a very profound example, but it is a good way to understand the principle. Of course, this can also have a much more intense effect.

Extreme attachment to one's own ideas about how things should and should not be can lead to crime and war. We are highly conditioned, full of hopes and fears that are created by personal and collective traumas, family systems, cultural beliefs, and so on.

Yes, we all know that. And how does it feel when these patterns disappear?

Free. When I am teaching, I often say: imagine you are walking through town in a new pair of shoes and the left one is too tight. Finally, you get home, and you can take it off – that is how it feels. One has a feeling of freedom, because there is no attachment anymore. Attachment is always connected to contraction, since one holds on to something or pushes it away. And this is always related to fear, which is the opposite of freedom.

How does one deal with emotions in mental training?
It is important to look at one's emotions with real interest, to direct goodwill towards oneself and to give it space, so that one can see which habitual tendencies have arisen in the mind. If one allows this self-healing process to happen, solutions will present themselves. Body and mind know how it works, but, without awareness and space, the transformation will not be able to take place.

Strong emotions, especially the ones you do not want, can become signposts. They can show you where you are. You can learn much by turning towards these entanglements with goodwill, without wishing to be somewhere else, that is, where those emotions no longer exist. An emotionally uncomfortable situation can be an opportunity to let go of the past, instead of endlessly repeating it. The most important thing is to not suppress these feelings and simply to let them be. One can only influence how one relates to current experiences, and, after all, emotions are impermanent – like everything else.

Personally, I tend to feel excluded very quickly. This comes from my experience of being the youngest family member, who was not allowed to join in, who could not do all the things her older siblings could already do. I know this, and yet I see this pattern again and again. Is it helpful simply to recognize the pattern?
Without a doubt! You say to yourself, this is interesting, what is going on here, what is this all about? You don't have to try to explain it to yourself; it is enough just to notice which bodily sensations, which feeling tones, and which mental states are present, together with the awareness that you are already familiar with this kind of mood. Scenarios that have

something to do with exclusion really resonate with you. Since there were situations in your past that have not yet been completely resolved, you are still easily hurt when they come up again.

However, with time it will get easier. The pattern will still be there, but it will not have so much power over you if you really befriend it and simply let it be, as it is. Often, we associate an uncomfortable feeling tone with the idea that something about ourselves or the situation is wrong. This is understandable but unrealistic. There can be many good things that are connected to unpleasant feeling tones. If you try to avoid discomfort, you will avoid growth.

Can you explain in more detail how to remain mindful if you find yourself in a maelstrom of emotions?
There are four establishments of mindfulness – the four satipatthana. This is the basic template for Buddhist meditation. *Sati* means 'mindfulness' or 'awareness', and *patthana* means something like 'training field'.

For an untrained mind, an experience seems like a huge tangle of countless different parts. One does not know where it begins and where it ends. Mindfulness allows us to recognize that this experience is indeed made up of different components. Taking apart an experience like this helps us to no longer identify with it so completely. Mindfulness means seeing what is really there, rather than losing oneself in a story one has made up about it.

The first training field is the body, *kaya*: what is happening at the physical level? For example, there is a sensation of pressure in my solar plexus, my hands are cold, and so on.

Then we proceed to the second level, feeling tones: how does it feel? Pleasant, unpleasant, or neutral?

The third level to be aware of is one's state of mind, the mood that colours the mind – for example, aversion and fear. Knowing that these influences are present is already very helpful, since I recognize that I am judging the whole situation through this filter, this veil.

This leads to the fourth level, principles of experience. Here we are concerned with recognizing interdependence, dependent origination. Here I see how conditioning works, and I can remind myself that everything that begins also ends. If I look after myself well in a difficult situation through this understanding and give my experience space, this is much more effective than distracting myself.

When you have lived through this process consciously a couple of times, then you will develop a deep trust in the fact that this state is actually also impermanent, and the attachment will automatically decrease. Attachment is simply a fear reaction – for example, the idea that a problematic situation will always remain like that. Do you understand this?

Yes. I have just realized that mindfulness can be practised at all four levels with a single experience.

While you are learning you can also take the levels separately. In a meditation, for example, you can train just mindfulness of the body. With beginners I usually start by teaching mindfulness at the bodily level, and then I give instructions about the other domains.

I keep coming back to this fundamental statement: it is not about what kind of an experience you have, but about how you relate to that experience. Experiences are never neutral: everyone sees things slightly differently, from their own point of view. Mindfulness means seeing how our intentions and actions manifest themselves in our body and in our mind. These intentions and actions are what propel us to the next birth, and the task here is to increasingly dissolve this momentum of the mind through insight.

With skills and talents that I like, I would prefer them to have permanent existence and not to dissolve.
But they do – nothing has permanent existence. And our good sides are simultaneously also our dark sides. For example, I am good at organizing things, but this contains an element of control that springs from fear. In my family I was the older sibling; my brother and I were often left alone, and I kept an eye on everything because I was afraid of what would happen if I did not. And I still try to keep an eye on everything today, if I am not mindful. Sixty years later, my brother lives somewhere completely different and yet I find myself doing the same in the monastery. In other words, the attachment is still there, but, compared to what it was decades ago, it has definitely decreased.

Buddhism in Daily Life

We have spoken at length about mental training in Buddhism. What are the visible aspects of Buddhist practice, the formal rituals?
I have used different types of practice in my life, sometimes very formal ones. However, over time my practice has become less and less complex, and more and more concerned with this one central question: what is the non-dualistic way of seeing my experiences? How can I accept my experience as it is, without making ego-centred value judgements? For me, recognizing whether there is attachment in the mind is at the core of Buddhist practice – recognizing attachment whenever it is there, and observing what it brings: suffering, confusion, and a clouding of the mind.

What kind of symbols and rituals were used in Early Buddhism and in your monastery?
Only a few compared to the Vajrayana, but it also depends how you look at it. We have a buddha statue and an image of Mahapajapati Gotami, the aunt and foster mother of the Buddha, who was one of the first bhikkhunis. There is also a statue of Prajnaparamita, the female embodiment of wisdom, which comes from the Mahayana. She is also described as the mother of all buddhas, since she symbolizes emptiness. In my room there are drawings of the bhikkhunis who were contemporaries of the historical Buddha and who were

mentioned by him by name in some of his discourses because of their outstanding qualities.

Community is a very important factor in our practice. Simply adhering to one's own individual programme can easily reinforce one's own egocentric tendencies.

At the monastery we follow a particular schedule: morning meditation, evening meditation, times of noble silence, and so on. After evening puja, there is noble silence until lunchtime on the following day, unless something urgent comes up. 'Puja' means something like 'devotion', and consists of chanting and meditation.

We chant recitations of the qualities of the Buddha, Dharma, and Sangha, discourses, summaries of discourses – for example, the five subjects for frequent recollection: I will get old, I will get ill, I will die, everything that is dear to me will be separated from me, and I am the heir to my actions.

We bow to the Buddha, Dharma, and Sangha, and in doing so remember the qualities about which we have already spoken in connection with the three refuges. This has an uplifting effect on the mind and makes it easier for the mind to open.

You also send a strong message through your outward appearance. What is the deeper meaning here?
The fact that I shave my head is a simplification. As a nun I do not need to worry about my hair. The shaved head is an unambiguous sign, part of my work clothing, if you want to call it that. It is also an ancient symbol for renunciation. As nuns we typically shave our heads on the day before the full moon and before the new moon; one can do it more or less often, but at least once a month.

Do you have special dietary restrictions?
We do not eat after noon, except for certain tonics or allowable substances such as cheese, dark chocolate, candied ginger, and soya milk. These correspond to the five tonics from the time of the Buddha that were used as medicine: honey, butter, ghee, molasses, and sugar. These were very expensive foods with a high calorie content.

The rule that states no solid food should be consumed after noon has a practical background. It ensured that alms mendicants did not appear at all times of day to collect food. Monks and nuns go through the village with their alms bowls very early in the morning, and then are not expected to be seen again until the following morning.

I have often seen you giving a blessing, for example before a meal or for a new home. What exactly are you doing there?
These are certain traditional chants and rituals used to try to allow good energy to flow into a situation. Monastics are asked to bless weddings or newborn babies, or are called to a deathbed for this purpose. Blessings are given to mark transitions. The linguistic root of the word 'blessing' is thought to be the same as that for the French word *blessure*, meaning 'wound' – an opening through which good energy or blessings can enter. One opens oneself to a transformation, although it also contains pain. I also give a blessing when you invite me to a meal, and rejoice in your generosity. It is all about recognizing that something has been given, and that dana or generosity is therefore being practised.

Before giving a blessing like this at a meal, you also ask who the merit should be shared with. In Buddhism the expression 'merit' comes up repeatedly. How should I understand this concept?

All intentional, wholesome actions involving the body, speech, and mind are meritorious. These are actions where you are thinking not only of yourself, but also of others, and of dependent origination. Each such action can also be dedicated to someone. For example, one can say, my grandmother died fifteen years ago today and I would like to dedicate the benefit of this meal offering to her, wherever she may be. This helps both people: it also helps the person who lost her grandmother, because she gets a sense that she can still do something good for her.

The first step towards making merit is dana, giving. Broadly speaking, the emphasis is on material generosity: giving away something of what you have. The next step is to cultivate the four divine abidings – loving-kindness, compassion, gladness, and equanimity – as basic attitudes towards yourself and the whole world. Merit manifests itself as more or less good conditions for practice, in your present as well as in future lives.

The opposite of merit is unwholesome action. The five precepts are there in order to give us boundaries within which fewer and fewer unwholesome actions take place. One could say that the quality of the mind is trained and changed in either a positive or a negative direction.

In other words, I can intentionally aim for the acquisition of merit, and in so doing work towards a better quality of life and a better rebirth. Is this not a contradiction in terms, if I do it egotistically for myself?

At the beginning it can involve a certain amount of self-interest, but this will dissipate as your practice progresses. Merit creates a positive impression on the mind, and so, just as practice develops on two levels, the mundane and the supermundane, there are two levels of merit. The worldly concept of merit – that is, comfortable circumstances – is a method for motivating people to practise. They follow the five precepts, live a good life, support other people who need support, protect people who need protection, and so on and so forth. This understanding of merit is mundane right view. People who practise in this way are known as 'householders'.

And then there is a second level at which merit can take effect, whereby you come to have more and more space around your experience and are thus increasingly able to dwell in awareness instead of identifying with your experience. This second level of merit is supermundane right view. It includes the intention to train the mind until complete liberation from greed, aversion, and delusion is achieved, which is described with the term 'nirvana'. 'Nirvana' literally means 'extinguishing', and is often also translated as 'awakening' or 'the unconditioned', 'the uncreated'.

Buddhist practice and the concept of merit therefore take place at two levels. At the worldly level, one recognizes that one has parents and children and obligations towards them, that one has received many things from other people, and that there is reciprocity. At the supermundane level, one practises to leave all ignorance behind, which ultimately ends in extinguishment.

Have you found any texts or lists particularly useful for Buddhist practice?
I find the thirty-seven *bodhipakkhiya-dhamma*[20] particularly useful. They represent the core structure of Early Buddhism, which repeatedly highlights the same thing, that is, the way to liberation. Imagine a jewel in the middle of a room with seven windows. You can look in through all seven windows and always see the same thing, but always from a different angle.

My favourite sutta is the *Dhammacakkappavattana Sutta*,[21] the first teaching of the Buddha, which set the wheel of Dharma in motion. In the first discourse he gave after his awakening, he addressed those five companions with whom he had practised for a long time, but who had left him after he had given up extreme ascetic practices. He called the path that he found the middle way, since it was the middle way between the two extremes. One extreme is to lose yourself in sensual pleasures, and the other is to castigate the body and not to give it what it needs. This middle way between the two extremes was first described in this teaching.

Are there any texts or discourses that are particularly helpful for women or that are particularly suitable for women? Is there something like a female practice in the teachings that have been written down?
No, there is nothing like that. From a Buddhist point of view, the concepts of sex and gender are seen as empty and not really existing. But, in daily life, some of the rules that apply to the bhikkhunis are different from those of the bhikkhus, the monks. Bhikkhunis were always in danger of being seen as 'fair game' and of being raped, and so they needed

protection. That brings us back to the two levels of Buddhist practice, which I have already discussed in connection with merit. It depends on what you are talking about: whether it is conventional existence, that is, daily life, or the way of realization. Ultimately all of these terms will become irrelevant, but, while we are still here and in these human bodies, we need to eat, we have passports, we are men, women, or something else.

There are lists in the canonical records, for example, of what distinguishes a good woman, a housekeeper. These lists were strongly influenced by the Iron Age culture of around 2,500 years ago. Women who lived in India at that time were the property of men, first of their fathers, then of their husbands, and, after their husbands had died, of their sons.

The *Therigatha* is a collection of poems that deal with awakening, written by the early nuns. These women who became nuns came from different social strata and lived at the time of the Buddha or slightly later. At the time it was considered very radical to allow a woman to leave the household and to support her as a nun. These women are fully awakened and were no different from the men of their time. Some parts of the *Therigatha* clearly address the fact that women have exactly the same potential as men.

For the first 500 years these texts – they are very poetic, and for this reason I prefer to describe them as poems – were passed on orally. The oldest existing transcriptions of the *Therigatha* are in the Pali Canon. These are so-called *Udanas*, inspired sayings that speak of the joy of being free and awakened in a surprisingly fresh and insightful way. They also include very detailed observations on the daily life of women in India at the time, which demonstrate a sharp awareness of human psychology, and account for the strong appeal that these texts have for contemporary readers. The *Therigatha* is one of the few Pali works that has found its way into modern world literature in numerous translations.

Is a teacher essential for Buddhist practice? Can one theoretically be a Buddhist and just rely on books?

I do not think one can understand Buddhism simply through books. In Early Buddhism and the Theravada it is said that someone who has entered the stream no longer needs a teacher. He or she has realized the first level of awakening, has already seen the Dharma, and therefore knows where he or she is headed. However, having a teacher would support and accelerate the journey towards full awakening.

In Buddhism the teacher plays an important role, and there are different ways in which a teacher can manifest. In Theravada the teacher is like a *kalyanamitta*, a friend who is further along the path than we are, who can help us and show us the way. One has obligations towards the teacher, but they are not considered infallible. In fact, it is the duty of the student to point it out, if they see that the teacher is making a mistake.

In later Buddhist traditions like the Vajrayana, one sees the teacher as a buddha and as infallible. Whatever they do is explained as being somehow beneficial for the student. This has a certain value, but things can also go wrong here, particularly in connection with sex, money, and power. Furthermore, it is difficult to get an overview of the situation, since one can only tell whether someone is fully awakened if one has reached that stage oneself. It is also difficult to maintain clarity because students as well as teachers bring their own projections.

One of the functions of the guru[22] is to bring things that are dormant into the light, and, in this respect, he or she is like a therapist. This is an important job, but when there are no control mechanisms it can be dangerous for the teacher and the student. A true guru, and these are rare, acts as a provocateur, as someone who challenges you, and at the same time as your protector, so that you do not get completely entangled and end up doing things that complicate your life. I have seen Buddhist practitioners from all schools who have totally lost the plot. When certain tendencies or traumas are touched, people can completely lose control. But the teacher can only protect you if there is true collaboration.

I know from my own experience how it feels to long for a teacher. My ideal would be for him or her to recognize me as a reincarnation, as an old acquaintance. I think I am not alone in wanting this.

This is a deeply feminine characteristic of patriarchy: you are recognized by the alpha male as the companion who is meant for him. I do not think that this is a problem that is particular to women. It belongs to the old patriarchal myths and patterns of thought that maintain the status quo and that in many respects are no longer appropriate for the world we live in today.

The patriarchal model of male dominance not only affects women and the feminine principle but also extends to the biosphere. One takes whatever one wants from the Earth regardless of loss. This approach has damaged the planet so badly that we will soon no longer be able to live here if we cannot find an adequate 'update' in time. My main concern is to support the necessary change in awareness so that future generations will be able to continue living here.

Do you also have male students?
Those who come to us mainly identify as women, but we have also drawn a diverse range of genders, including men and trans people. There are bhikkhunis who are described as female in their passports but who do not experience themselves as either female or male. I have also noticed that gay men tend to be more open to a wide range of Dharma expressions, including feminine voices. In the more recent teacher-training programmes at Spirit Rock and IMS, efforts were made to invite people of colour, trans people, and queer people. They are currently being particularly encouraged, so that the body of Buddhist teachers is in a better position to reflect contemporary society. The teaching of Buddhism has to become more diverse – this is a big topic, not just in the United States.

You just mentioned the feminine ways in which the Buddha's teachings are expressed. What does this comprise?
It would be very hard to generalize about that. Perhaps it is about a greater capacity to deal with emotions and to name them. Women tend to place less emphasis on hierarchy and make more of an effort to treat each other as equals. However, there is always a certain hierarchy in monasteries. Someone who has been ordained for longer will often have more experience and therefore more to say. There are also

bhikkhuni communities that stick closely to traditional Asian models, where hierarchy is quite strongly emphasized.

This might be a strange question, but what might a world look like in which everyone is awakened?
It is pointless to try to imagine this. All sentient beings on this planet experience their existence differently because they all look through different filters. Each one lives in their own world. For those who are fully awakened there is no longer any volition in the mind stream and it goes out – it ends. All others will continue to move through unfolding lifetimes until they see that the only way to true peace and fulfilment is by no longer wanting.

For a long time, our sciences were based on the assumption that there is an objective world, a single actual world. But outside the six senses there is no world. This does not mean that there is nothing there – of course there is. But there is much more than just your perspective or mine. For example, a chameleon sees everything quite differently from us. Forty different types of eye have emerged over the course of evolution, and they all see the world in their own particular ways.

Where is the reward in Buddhist practice? There are some religious movements where people pray to win the lottery on the following weekend. There is no immediate gratification on the Buddhist path.
In all religions there are different levels of practice, because there are so many different people, and this is no different in Buddhism. Here, too, you can go to a monk and get your daughter's fountain pen blessed to bring her luck in an exam, or the car you have just bought, or the house you have just moved into.

At a more mature level, religious practice becomes less and less self-centred. At the beginning I might still be concerned about passing my exam, giving birth to a son, being healthy. But then my practice becomes more and more refined, and at some point the only thing that I still want is that my actions be of benefit to others, because this makes me happy. In other words, one becomes increasingly aware that one's own happiness is connected to the happiness of others, and that one cannot be happy by oneself.

Wisdom and compassion are like two sides of the same coin. If something is truly wise, then there is compassion there; if there is true compassion, it can only be enacted through wisdom. True compassion and true wisdom always arise together.

What Are You Waiting For? Buddhism Here and Now

Buddhism is over 2,500 years old. What can it teach the world today?
It has the same liberating power as it did in Iron Age India 2,500 years ago. Buddhism is a path towards freedom from ignorance and therefore also freedom from stress and suffering. You can take as much of it as you want or can handle. You can lead a less stressful life, because you respond to experiences in a wholesome way, or you can go all the way to full awakening or extinguishing, or stop at any stage in between. The end of samsara can only be experienced individually. Whether a person lives in samsara or nirvana depends on their mental and emotional filters; there is no end to samsara per se.

Today, all the people on the planet have the same problem with respect to the limits of the biosphere. The greatest material challenge that humanity has ever had to face is simultaneously also a unique possibility for us to take the next evolutionary step as a species. Everything that has to happen on this planet in order for us to survive can also support the maturing of our species. In Buddhism as well as in other spiritual systems, life is seen not as an opportunity to experience more comfortable things and fewer uncomfortable ones, but as a chance to learn.

The climate crisis can help us recognize what serious consequences our delusions can have. It is a problem created by *Homo sapiens*. It is no small thing to acknowledge how important it is that you work on your own development, not just for you, your husband, your wife, and your family, but for the whole global community, plants and animals included, for everything.

In your experience, what leads people to Buddhism today? What are the people who come to you seeking?

Buddhism is very pragmatic. You might come to my talk, receive guidance on meditation, and then we might meditate together. After that, you might practise meditation alone every day for twenty minutes or so, and over time you will experience real success in the form of insights. Perhaps not success: let us rather say you have learned a skill that you can continue to develop over time.

In Buddhism you do not need to believe in anything in particular or sign up to anything. You only have to invest time in order to try it for yourself. The only instructions, in my opinion, that should be followed as closely as possible from the beginning are the five precepts. But you will probably discover this for yourself. When you meditate, you become sensitized, so that you no longer want to do certain things or are no longer able to do them.

In wider society people are starting to recognize that they can work with their mind, that they are not just passive victims of their own mind. This is closely connected to the findings of psychology, especially in the area of brain plasticity. People have realized that there are different ways and means of systematically transforming the mind, and Buddhism is one of them. Buddhists have been doing this for more than 2,500 years.

Different people have different motives for doing things. Some of them might be motivated by the fact that it is hip to meditate, and because it is really cool to learn this skill from a nun. Others might have a genuine interest in authentic teachings, for example those of Early Buddhism, and really want to know what the essence of those teachings is.

When you talk about mental transformation, I still do not fully understand you. What happens in the mind and what remains when I die, when my body decays?
In general, we believe in a self, in some sort of core that is our self. But, in reality, the mind is a river that is changing every moment. And at some point, the body, which is actually also a river or a process that only flows with the river of the mind for a certain time, becomes so old or ill that it dies, dissolves, and disappears. The elements that have given the body shape return to the elements that they originally came from. Earth to earth, water to water, and so on.

If the river of the mind is not wholly free from wanting and doing, then it will take a new body for the next life. A practitioner dies and then simply carries on where they left off in the next life. If the practice has become imprinted in the mind really well, then they will remember it much more quickly and will also be born into circumstances in which there is support for their practice.

Speech is dualistic: we tend to speak only of being or notbeing. If you look at photos of your childhood, for example, you might see yourself in the living room of your parents' house. Is that really you? Neither is it you nor is it *not* you: the river simply flowed on. Someone who understands this point does not even ask questions like this anymore. They know that one cannot really answer such questions at the intellectual level.

I think there is a basic difference in comprehension here between Eastern and Western philosophy. Aristotelian logic, which characterizes our thinking today, is based on the concept of exclusion, of yes or no.

This is also one reason why Buddhism offers something that people here in the West thirst for. Western philosophy is grounded in yes or no. With this type of thinking, people have accomplished and created many things, including powerful computers.

But there is more to it, the so-called grey zone, which is seen as something secondary or half-baked. We reluctantly accept that the mind can continue to develop and open up to other dimensions that we cannot even describe using conventional language, and that is why we call it the grey zone.

Are there actually two rivers of consciousness? The one that flows through me, that always contains a part of me, and then another general one, containing everything surrounding me?

The Buddha always answered questions like this by saying: you do not need to worry your head about this. Work on what you are actually experiencing right now, and the rest will become clear. If one always wants to know everything, it can be an excuse not to meditate, because one needs to clarify this or that beforehand. If you meditate and really address what is happening in your mind, then presumably you will come across a good portion of unprocessed feelings. Some people prefer to stay inside their mind without ever truly practising, which gives them a sense of control.

Buddhism is a minority interest, at least in Europe and the United States. Could one say it is elite?

It must be said that people who convert to Buddhism in the West are usually people from the white middle class. That is why programmes to promote diversity in Buddhism are being so strongly encouraged in the United States right now.

In Asia there are many Buddhists who cannot read or write. So to say that Buddhism is difficult to understand or to communicate is simply untrue. But coming back to Europe and the United States: middle-class people have money. They have already been able to fulfil some of their basic needs and therefore recognize that satisfying only material needs is not truly fulfilling; then they come across a teaching that clearly states that everything is unsatisfactory. For people who have not yet been able to fulfil enough of their immediate, material needs, it may be more difficult to come to the realization that everything is unsatisfactory. The fact that Buddhism has not been adopted on a large scale in Europe can also be explained by the fact that in Buddhism there is no anthropomorphic God. According to patriarchal patterns of thinking, when one is afraid, one wants a powerful man with a beard who will tell one which way to go. There is nobody like this in Buddhism. There is no God per se, but there is the Dharma. This also corresponds to a court of final instance, but it is not populated by people. Dharma is the laws of nature: however you treat others, that is how you will be treated in return. This is cause and effect in a world in which everything has arisen interdependently.

People say that Buddhism adapts well to different cultural conditions or contemporary circumstances. Where do you see the greatest challenges today?

There are certain areas with significant scope for adaptation. I have the greatest respect for the different transmission lineages that have all come from Asia, yet at the same time I think that it would be appropriate to translate these very pragmatic and liberating teachings into the images and languages of our own cultures in Europe and the United States. This is something that interests me particularly, and I think that my background in social and cultural anthropology and my experience with theatre and performance would stand me in good stead in this area.

How would you explain in a few words to someone who knows little about Buddhism why they should become a Buddhist?

I would never tell anyone that they should become a Buddhist. I would recommend that they take the time, for example, to listen to some basic meditation guidance and then see if it makes sense to them or not. One becomes a Buddhist when one has become convinced to a certain degree that the teachings are beneficial, that they are essentially of benefit. Everyone has to experience this for themselves, in order to be able to decide.

I do not see it as my duty to turn people into Buddhists at all. If someone wants to learn something from me, then they can come. I try not just to teach the Dharma but also to live it. Some people feel drawn to this, and others might think: what is so special about this nun? It is as simple as that.

I read somewhere that it is considered to be of the greatest merit in Buddhism to bring another person into contact with Buddhist teaching. Isn't there something missionary about this?

This is true, but at the same time we do not set out to be missionaries. As a European I would even say that it does not have to be the Buddha's teaching, but rather some kind of spiritual path that leads to freedom, wisdom, and compassion. I understood the elements of the Buddhist path very quickly and was soon quite convinced that they were all consistent. But presumably I did some preparation in a previous life!

You can organize a Dharma day, give someone a Dharma book that you like, and so on. But what that person does when they come into contact with the Buddha's teachings, that is something they alone should be in charge of.

What if I ask you for advice about beginning my practice as a Buddhist?

Simply begin! What are you waiting for? By getting started you will acquire personal experience that will generate its own momentum, and so it just carries on. The three refuges are a kind of navigation system. If you have no ideals, no vision, and no goals, you will get lost and go round in circles. At the same time, you need to keep your eyes on the road, in case there is a pothole or some other obstacle there. You need to keep your eye on both things at once: that is the middle way.

The Next Steps on the Path:
Santacitta Bhikkhuni Explains the Aloka Earth Room Concept

Aloka Earth Room is a contemporary temple-space interweaving Dharma, ecology, and art based in San Rafael, California. It is an attempt to unite the Buddha's teachings with an awareness of the Earth and our true place within it ('Earth awareness'). The Earth, as a self-regenerating, intelligent being, has known for more than 4.5 billion years how to sustain life. As the dominant species, we humans and our impact are increasingly disrupting the equilibrium of the planet as we know it. We are witnessing a mass extinction of more-than-human species, an increasing loss of habitat, and a massive exploitation of so-called natural resources. Through language and the written word, the way in which we use language, our upbringing, and the cultural assumptions that it entails, humanity is suffering a crisis of perception. We experience ourselves as separate from the Earth and presume to live on the planet like performers on a stage. We walk up and down on it, take what we want and discard what we do not. But, in reality, we are a part of the biosphere, we do not live 'on' but rather 'in' the planet.

We urgently need to wake up and acknowledge that we share the Earth with many millions of other species, and, in so doing, find our true place in this delicate web of life. The Earth is a powerful teacher: the biosphere can teach us in a direct manner what emptiness is.[23]

The Earth Room provides support for the development of such Earth awareness. I see the space as a kind of healing architecture that is designed to reflect, for practitioners, where the heart and mind need to go. The Earth Room shares this with churches, temples, and other sacred architecture. For example, Gothic cathedrals support the transcendence of the mind. In the Earth Room, by contrast, the whole person is inspired to feel the Earth as the indisputable basis of their existence. Consciousness can be prompted by particular meditation instructions to experience and stabilize this kind of expansion of perception. My first teacher, Ajahn Buddhadasa, often said that the laws of nature will take care of us if we make the effort to cooperate with nature instead of working against it. This is a process, and it is more about the *how* than about the *what*. If we make space in ourselves, then wisdom can manifest; if we act according to what is true for us, then we will become truly alive – creativity will be awakened, and the unexpected will occur. A crisis has the potential to generate change and renewal and to release powerful energies. A crisis can bring people together and lead them to achieve what they might once have considered impossible.

What is critical is how we deal with not-knowing and darkness, when it is unclear how we should proceed. Can we keep this space of uncertainty open, or do we need to fill it up with activity immediately? If we have faith in natural processes and the intelligence of life itself, if we orientate ourselves towards the Earth, then the transformation necessary for the evolution of humankind will take place. If we orientate ourselves towards our intellect alone, we cannot succeed.

Santacitta Bhikkhuni Explains the Aloka Earth Room Concept

The way to escape samsara is the noble eightfold path,[24] and in our present age this path also leads through service to the regeneration of the Earth. This has become a part of the path: participating in the regeneration of the Earth, supporting the self-regeneration of the biosphere. And this will be achieved not by developing more technology, but rather through remembering our ancient capacity for living in coexistence and cooperation with the planet. In so doing, we ground our intellectual achievements within the ecological boundaries for life on this planet. Anything that is aloof and separate from the Earth will not prosper but will dry up and wither away, because it is not connected to the vitality that takes place in the biosphere.

After living and working in Buddhist monasteries for more than thirty years, I have decided to temporarily withdraw from living in community in order to develop the Aloka Earth Room. I continue to maintain contact with several Buddhist monasteries, but for the design of the Earth Room I am solely responsible.

In the Earth Room we learn together to sense our deep embeddedness in the web of life. Through simple rituals and discussions and by sitting in council, we deepen these experiences together. Fears, uncertainties, and worries are discussed, processed, and integrated, allowing the intelligence of the Earth to shine through more and more. This is a multigenerational undertaking, and the container of the Earth Room is designed in such a way as to support this process.

There are still humans today who live in deliberately cultivated cooperation with the Earth. Indigenous nations comprise around 6 per cent of the global population and steward around 80 per cent of the remaining biodiversity. A deep connection with the land and the respect that this engenders are expressed through observances that are part of daily life. For example, permission is sought before something is taken from the Earth or before an animal is killed. The preservation of traditions and the passing on of rituals are simply there to keep life going, and, in this respect, they can be compared to art.

I am still only just beginning to find rituals for Earth awareness. The basic ingredients of rituals are the same everywhere: asking for permission, some sort of offering, a request, deep listening, and giving thanks. Beauty plays an important role in all of this. As a native European, my ancestry includes indigenous people in the distant past. My indigenous predecessors were persecuted in the Middle Ages, when modern science attempted to wipe out the guardians of the ancient, Earth-based healing arts.

As a nun, my experience as artist and anthropologist helps me to trust in the process of emergence, to rely on the fact that the details of the design will come through experimentation. This is what the prototype of the first Earth Room is all about, and this is my particular intention here in San Rafael: I would like to demonstrate what an Earth Room can be like.

The Buddha's teachings are all about liberating the heart and mind from ignorance and delusion. Art can be instrumental in this process: it can open the heart and expand the mind, so that broader interconnections can be recognized. This enables us to let go of conditioned, limiting patterns and filters that have been acquired.

Art is like an oil that lubricates the wheels of this process. In designing the Earth Room, my intention is to provide a space in which the immanent intelligence of the Earth can be sensed. The Earth Room is an installation and reminds us, like a walk-in altar, that it is time to develop Earth awareness. When we have a new perspective or a new concept directly before our eyes, and perhaps can even touch it, a more intimate connection with our inner processes occurs, enabling us to integrate our insights more smoothly. Objects on an altar stand for particular qualities and ideas that cannot be expressed in words, or that are not yet fully formed. When these new ideas are made tangible in this way, the development of our inner processes is fuelled. For me, an altar can have a similar function to a to-do list: it saves me from having to keep everything in my head. When I see the objects on my altar, I sense something and I remember. Applied symbolism supercharges human evolution and has been used for this purpose for thousands of years.

The development of the Earth Room is a gradual, creative process. The current location in a quiet cul-de-sac here in San Rafael is a kind of incubator for the idea. Since its opening in April 2023, the original concept has become sufficiently stable to be implemented on a larger scale. This will be the next step for the Earth Room as an emerging, healing architecture.

Appendix 1
Biography of Santacitta Bhikkhuni

Santacitta Bhikkhuni was born Sylvia Helga Bayer in Bruck an der Mur in Styria, Austria. She was the first child of the owners of the Hotel Restaurant Bayer on the main square of the small town. Her brother was born a year later. Their parents were affectionate towards Sylvia and her brother to the extent their work permitted. However, the children only seldom enjoyed their parents' undivided attention, since family life took place in the hotel.

Every winter the family went on journeys that were very adventurous by the standards of the time, and that made a deep impression on the children. In Gran Canaria, thirteen-year-old Sylvia and her brother had a close brush with death, almost drowning in the wintry Atlantic.

In the years that followed, the family visited Africa several times, and new horizons opened up for Sylvia.

Her parents were culturally Catholic, but Sylvia and her brother did not experience any religious pressure from their family. For their parents it was a foregone conclusion that one of the two children would later take over the hotel, possibly even the daughter. Consequently, after completing her compulsory education in 1975, Sylvia attended a hotel-management school in Bad Gleichenberg, also in Styria. Subsequently she graduated from the Institute of Higher Education in Tourism in Schloss Klessheim in Salzburg, although she did not plan to work in this sector.

In 1979 Sylvia moved to Vienna and her world opened up

further. She began studying ethnology, which is today referred to as cultural and social anthropology. Her partner, whom she met at the hotel-management school, was a member of a theatre company run by Erwin Piplits and Ulrike Kaufmann, who worked with masks and puppets; in 1980 this became the avant-garde Serapionstheater, which would later gain international renown. Alongside her studies, Sylvia worked at the Serapionstheater in the cloakroom and at the box office, and was able to demonstrate her creativity and craftsmanship in the design and creation of costumes.

After several relocations within Vienna, Sylvia and her partner moved to Maria Lanzendorf in Lower Austria, where they co-founded the Ökotopisches Zentrum with a group of friends.

In 1982 she began to work as a performer at the Serapionstheater. She had her stage debut in the production *Double and Paradise,* the first production to take the ensemble's success outside Austria. Following the end of her relationship with her partner, she left Maria Lanzendorf and moved into a shared flat with two fellow students in Vienna. However, it proved difficult to combine her studies with her theatre activities in the longer term, and in 1985 she left the ensemble in order to finish writing her dissertation, which also focused on dance, rituals, and symbols. She found it hard to leave the theatre; to supplement her income she then worked as a waitress in the Bermuda Triangle nightlife district of Vienna.

In 1986 her mother died following a riding accident, and a year later Sylvia travelled to Thailand and came into contact with Buddhism for the first time. She fell in love with a young fisherman on the island of Ko Phi Phi; on her return to Vienna she changed the topic of her dissertation, planning to carry out fieldwork on the subject of dance and ritual in Thailand.

Back in Thailand, following a chance encounter in 1988, she visited Wat Suan Mokkh, a forest monastery led by Ajahn Buddhadasa, and learned to meditate. Her young lover died of a drug overdose on a trip to North Thailand; following a traffic accident shortly afterwards, Sylvia returned to Austria for one year, working at the family hotel that had now been taken over by her brother.

In 1989 she travelled to Thailand again and worked as a customer relations manager for an Austrian travel agent, intending to build up a professional career in tourism in Thailand. In 1990 she married her local business partner, who later turned out to be a criminal who was involved in the tourism mafia. She made regular visits back to Suan Mokkh monastery, and after a year and a half managed to divorce her Thai husband.

In 1991 she moved into Suan Mokkh, the monastery of her first Buddhist teacher Ajahn Buddhadasa, although at this point she did not yet intend to live in a monastery permanently.

In autumn 1992 she visited Amaravati monastery near London, England, a monastery in the Ajahn Chah lineage of the Thai Forest Tradition. After staying there for ten months she was ordained as an anagarika[25] ('homeless one') in June 1993. As an anagarika she shaved her head, wore white robes, and lived at the monastery permanently. She received training and instruction, and worked mainly in the kitchen where a small team cooked all the meals for forty to sixty people. The community at Amaravati was international, and men and women from more than twenty countries lived there under the spiritual guidance of Ajahn Sumedho, who had been sent to England by Ajahn Chah in 1977.

In 1995 she travelled with a senior nun from Amaravati through Australia to Thailand, and then on to the United States. In Thailand she lived with nuns in various monasteries of the Ajahn Chah lineage, returning to Amaravati in 1997.

In 1998 Sylvia was ordained as a siladhara[26] and received the name Santacitta, meaning 'peaceful heart-mind', from Ajahn Sumedho. The longer she spent living and training as part of the community at Amaravati, the more she became aware of the limitations that were placed on her there as a woman.

In 2002, at a Kalachakra ceremony with His Holiness the Dalai Lama in Graz, she met her Vajrayana teacher Shechen Rabjam Rinpoche, abbot of the Shechen monastery in Kathmandu and distinguished teacher of the Nyingma School of Tibetan Buddhism.

In 2004 Santacitta set off on a pilgrimage to India and Nepal with a friend, visiting historic Buddhist places and finally Shechen, the monastery of her Tibetan teacher. She found herself increasingly interested in Tibetan Buddhism.

In 2008, Santacitta, who was now a teaching nun (ajahn) at Amaravati, travelled to the United States with Ajahn Anandabodhi, a fellow sister from Amaravati, in order to explore the possibilities for establishing a branch monastery for women. Aloka Vihara ('realm of light or awareness') was opened in San Francisco in December of the following year. Ajahn Santacitta and Ajahn Anandabodhi decided to leave the Ajahn Chah lineage in April 2011, and were ordained as bhikkhunis at Spirit Rock in October 2011.

In 2014 the community relocated to the hinterland of San Francisco, to a forested area in the Sierra Nevada foothills, and opened the Aloka Vihara forest monastery, co-led by Ayya Santacitta and Ayya Anandabodhi. Ayya Santacitta became involved not only in the empowerment of women but also in the environmental movement, and received international recognition for her engagement three times.

Due to the increasing number of forest fires in California, the Aloka Vihara monastic community decided to leave the property in the hinterland of San Francisco in autumn 2022. Subsequently Ayya Santacitta founded the Aloka Earth Room, a contemporary temple-space interweaving Dharma, ecology, and art, in San Rafael, around thirty kilometres north of San Francisco. Aloka Earth Room is inspired by Ajahn Buddhadasa's Spiritual Theatre in Wat Suan Mokkh, Thailand.

The bhikkhunis of the former Aloka Vihara forest monastery do not belong to any of the lineages of the Thai Forest Tradition that were founded by famous monks during the last century. The Theravada bhikkhuni communities of today are still young and well networked among themselves. It is possible that, in the future, people will speak about what the bhikkhunis are currently developing not as a lineage but as a circle.

Information about the activities of Ayya Santacitta is available at https://alokavihara.org/.

Appendix 2
Short Biography of Irmgard Kirchner

Irmgard Kirchner was born in 1959 in Innsbruck in Tyrol, Austria. She spent her childhood in a small village in the Tyrolean mountains, and after leaving school moved to Vienna in order to study cultural anthropology (then known as ethnology) and psychology. After finishing her degree, she turned the skills that she had learned in the course of her studies – that is, how to carry out research, speak to people, listen, and ask relevant questions – into a lifelong career.

Following more than twenty years as editor in chief of *Südwind*, a magazine devoted to international politics, culture, and development, she still devotes herself to writing today, except when she is watching insects and birds in the wildlife haven that is her garden.

Appendix 3
Short Biography of Gwen Clayton

Gwen Clayton was born in 1971 in Cambridge, England. She grew up in Canton Thurgau and Cambridge, and spent many happy childhood holidays visiting her German grandparents in the Black Forest. She read Japanese studies at the University of Oxford, then trained as a solicitor, working in commercial law firms in London, Tokyo, and Zurich. She has been active as a professional translator for the last sixteen years, specializing in law and the humanities. For further details, please see www.perfectlyphrased.com.

Appendix 4

Bhikkhuni Ordination in the Theravada Tradition of Buddhism: A Conversation between Irmgard Kirchner and Ute Hüsken, Professor of South Asian Cultural and Religious History at the University of Heidelberg

Could you briefly explain the significance of bhikkhuni ordination in the Theravada tradition of Buddhism?

According to tradition, the Buddha himself established the bhikkhu sangha, the order of monks, and a little later also the bhikkhuni sangha, the order of nuns. This is the same across all of the Buddhist traditions. The bhikkhuni sangha must have existed for hundreds of years. We know this through texts, through inscriptions, and through external written documents and records.

At some point the ordination lineage was interrupted and the bhikkhuni sangha died out in the Theravada tradition. This would have happened at different times in different places. In Sri Lanka one can date it to around the twelfth century. In India the bhikkhuni sangha cannot have survived for much longer. We do not really know why this happened; we only know that it did.

This fact presents the Theravada tradition with a problem, since, according to Buddhist tradition, everyone who is ordained – whether a monk or a nun – must be able to trace their ordination lineage back to the Buddha himself.

The Buddha must be present somewhere in the long line of ordination mothers and ordination fathers, if we want to use those expressions. This means that, when an ordination tradition has died out or has been interrupted, then the question of whether it can be re-established is debatable. There seem to have been no fully ordained nuns in the Theravada tradition for several centuries, at least none that we know of.

What does 'fully ordained' mean?
If someone is fully ordained, it means they have undergone a particular ceremony and have been accepted by the members of an order as a full member of that order themselves. This involves, among other things, the wearing of special clothing – in the Theravada tradition, orange or ochre-coloured robes – and shaving one's head. Above all, those who have been fully ordained take it upon themselves to follow the rules that apply to Buddhist monks and nuns in the Theravada tradition. From the Buddhist perspective this is a legal act: they step outside the world of people who have a dwelling, and become someone who is houseless. They no longer have a permanent residence.

The process of ordination is important and follows particular rules. It is a ceremony, a ritual, one might also call it an initiation. When we consider the question of whether the order of nuns can be re-established, these rules play an important role, both for those who are in favour of a re-establishment of the bhikkhuni sangha and for those who oppose it.

Some of the canonical texts attributed to the Buddha are nearly 2,500 years old. They include passages stipulating that the ordination of a bhikkhuni should first be performed by the nuns and then be approved by the monks. In other words, both sanghas are required for a nun to be legitimately ordained.

Naturally this is difficult when nuns' orders no longer exist. For conservative circles in and around the Theravada order, this is a central argument for not being able to ordain any nuns – simply because there is no nuns' sangha.

There are currently some fully ordained bhikkhunis – how did they manage to become ordained?

Those who are currently bhikkhunis became bhikkhunis in very different ways. One is through a different interpretation of the same texts. The texts have been passed on over 2,500 years, and have also been compiled by different people. In some places they are bound to have been changed. In those texts that describe the first ordinations of women, we also see a development. The first woman to be ordained is the foster mother of the Buddha, Mahapajapati Gotami, who asks her son for the ordination herself. He grants this, according to the texts, at any rate after a few requests. She becomes ordained in such a way that her son, the historical Buddha, accepts her into the order. She is followed by her fellowship, the 500 women with whom she walked to Vaishali to be ordained by her son. These women are then ordained by monks.

This means that there are definitely historical precedents, at least if we follow the texts, where nuns are ordained not by nuns and monks but only by monks. This is an important argument for those who say that we do not necessarily need nuns for an ordination, if there is no order of nuns; after all, at the beginning there were no nuns, only monks.

Which other ways are there?

Some of the early ordinations that have taken place in our time were carried out with the help of nuns from other Buddhist traditions, with nuns from the Mahayana tradition. Of course, these nuns can trace their line back to the Buddha.

And here is a further argument: in the fourth century CE, a delegation of Theravada nuns travelled to China and established the ordination of nuns there. One can thus argue that the Chinese ordination of nuns also comes from Sri Lanka, and it would therefore be legitimate and legally valid if Chinese nuns now went back to Sri Lanka or other countries where there is Theravada Buddhism and helped in the ordination of women there.

Are there still nuns with unbroken ordination lineages in other Buddhist traditions?

Yes. In the Mahayana tradition – for example, in China and Taiwan – there are nuns who see themselves as belonging to an uninterrupted lineage. People are divided on the question of whether there have ever been fully ordained nuns in the Tibetan tradition. There have been important female Buddhist teachers, but whether or not we can speak of them as nuns who are equivalent to bhikkhunis is questionable.

Since when have there been attempts in the Theravada tradition of Buddhism to reintroduce bhikkhuni ordination in one way or another?

These attempts began in the 1980s and have been very intense since the mid-1990s. In the meantime, a second and third generation of bhikkhunis have already been ordained. It is therefore fair to say that the bhikkhuni sangha has been reintroduced into the Theravada tradition. It is interesting to note that this has been a very international movement since the beginning.

Women from Asia have been involved, for example, women from Sri Lanka and India, as well as women from the West, for example, from Germany and the United States. It was an endeavour that went beyond national borders, which is good, but this also brought its own problems. The traditions of different countries are simply different, and there were discussions about the details, but the efforts have been very successful in any event. I get the impression that the Theravada tradition appeals to many women today, and there is now a long line of women being, as it were, reordained from the Mahayana to the Theravada tradition in order to join these bhikkhuni sanghas.

Is it possible to say how many bhikkhunis there are compared to the monks, the bhikkhus, in the Theravada tradition?
Not for me, at any rate. It really depends on the country. In Thailand and Myanmar, for example, the conservative powers that speak out against the ordination of women are so strong that there is a prohibition on women being ordained. But, at the same time, there are already several groups of bhikkhuni sanghas in Thailand, where women live and practise as nuns even though they were not able to get ordained in that country. For this purpose they usually go to Sri Lanka.

The number of bhikkhunis is growing. The availability of educational and training facilities for nuns – above all in Sri Lanka – has played a particularly important role here. The path to ordination is becoming increasingly established and increasingly normal.

Could you explain what you mean by 'conservative powers'?
I mean, in particular, groups of monks who are against bhikkhuni ordination, but there are also opponents among lay Buddhists who materially support the sangha. I consider the notion that the ordination of women cannot take place to be a conservative one.

But it should be stressed that there have also been monks from the start who have supported bhikkhuni ordination. Some of them are very prominent: they carry out academic research on the topic and demonstrate that the ordination of women is also possible under monastic law.

The fact that monks and nuns as well as laypeople are needed for a complete sangha is acknowledged by all the schools of Buddhism. Nevertheless, there are orders, like the Ajahn Chah lineage, with numerous Western monks in leadership positions, which continue to adhere to the position that bhikkhuni ordination is not possible. What is the problem with re-establishing bhikkhuni ordination? Are there patriarchal interests at work here?

It depends, and the issue needs to be considered on a case-by-case basis, but naturally the first explanation that comes to mind is that opponents of bhikkhuni ordination are trying to prevent competing organizations from establishing themselves in the first place. In many South and South-East Asian countries, the decision to become a monk is not necessarily made on a voluntary basis. It is possible for a family to give one of their sons to a monastery; a poor family might not see any other options. After all, Buddhist monasteries offer training, board, and lodging. Joining an order on the basis of religious conviction is more the exception than the rule in many countries where there is Theravada Buddhism.

Nuns, by contrast, often have to overcome significant obstacles before they can enter a monastery, and yet that is where they really want to be. Their attitude is usually completely different. As a result, nuns usually have a good reputation: they take what they do seriously, because they do it out of conviction. One of the duties fulfilled by monks and nuns is to carry out rituals that accompany transition points in the human life cycle. It is much more pleasant and popular with families to invite ritual specialists who do this wholeheartedly.

And that is why there is competition?
Yes. I would say so.

You spoke of the second and third generation of bhikkhunis to be ordained in the Theravada tradition. Where does Ayya Santacitta fit into this picture?
In the first generation, from a monastic-law perspective. This first generation not only re-established full ordination, they also campaigned heavily so that the bhikkhuni sangha could develop and grow. This was not done independently of, but rather in conformity with, monastic law, so that anyone who had any doubt could come on board. This was and continues to be an important objective, and is also the reason why these efforts have been so successful.

The first generation is inevitably made up of women who are unafraid of resistance. These women had to be leaders but also had to have charisma, otherwise they could not have taken anyone with them.

What does the re-establishment of bhikkhuni ordination have to do with Western feminism?

Many of the first Theravada nuns who presided at bhikkhuni ordinations were nuns from Sri Lanka, but bhikkhuni sanghas around the world are very diverse. Women from South-East Asia, South Asia, and more recently East Asia and the West all live and practise together. To dismiss this as quasi-Western feminism is easy, and to refute it is hard, but the label is not really appropriate.

Just as in every group, there are very different people with very different interests. Nuns do not necessarily hug each other all the time. There are also internal disagreements about where all this is going, and this is a good thing. Do I want to copy the way things were done in northern India 2,500 years ago? What do I want to use my practice, my insights, and my opportunities for? The answers to these questions will inevitably be very different.

Appendix 5

Thirty-Seven Qualities That Inspire Awakening (*bodhipakkhiya-dhamma*)[27]

I. The four establishments of mindfulness (*satipatthana*)

1. Contemplation of body (*kayanupassana*)
2. Contemplation of feelings (*vedananupassana*)
3. Contemplation of mind (*cittanupassana*)
4. Contemplation of categories of phenomena/experience (*dhammanupassana*)

II. The four right efforts (*samma-padhana*)

1. Effort to prevent unskilful states from arising (*samvara-padhana*)
2. Effort to abandon and dissolve unskilful states that have already arisen (*pahana-padhana*)
3. Effort to arouse skilful states (*bhavana-padhana*)
4. Effort to sustain and develop skilful states that have already arisen (*anurakkhana-padhana*)

III. The four roads to power (*iddhipada*)

1. Will/striving/intention (*chanda-iddhipada*)
2. Energy/perseverance/courage (*viriya-iddhipada*)
3. Integration/order (*citta-iddhipada*)
4. Investigation/consideration/attunement (*vimamsa-iddhipada*)

IV. The five spiritual faculties (*indriya*)

1. Faith/trust/confidence (*saddha*)
2. Energy (*viriya*)
3. Mindfulness/awareness (*sati*)
4. Stability/collectedness (*samadhi*)
5. Wisdom/insight (*panna*)

V. The five strengths (*bala*)

1. Faith/trust/confidence (*saddha*)
2. Energy (*viriya*)
3. Mindfulness/awareness (*sati*)
4. Stability/collectedness (*samadhi*)
5. Wisdom/insight (*panna*)

VI. The seven awakening factors (*bojjhanga*)

1. Mindfulness (*sati-sambojjhanga*)
2. Investigation (*dhammavicaya-sambojjhanga*)
3. Energy (*viriya-sambojjhanga*)
4. Joy (*piti-sambojjhanga*)
5. Tranquillity (*passaddhi-sambojjhanga*)
6. Stability/collectedness (*samadhi-sambojjhanga*)
7. Equipoise (*upekkha-sambojjhanga*)

VII. The noble eightfold path (*ariya atthangika magga*)

1. Right view (*samma-ditthi*)
2. Right intention (*samma-sankappa*)
3. Right speech (*samma-vaca*)
4. Right action (*samma-kammanta*)

5. Right livelihood (*samma-ajiva*)
6. Right effort (*samma-vayama*)
7. Right mindfulness (*samma-sati*)
8. Right stability/collectedness (*samma-samadhi*)

Notes

1 Pali: Ayya.
2 An internationally successful avant-garde theatre group founded by Ulrike Kaufmann and Erwin Piplits in Vienna in 1973, which still runs its own theatre today, www.odeon-theater.at.
3 Ajahn Buddhadasa (1906–93) was one of the most influential monks of Theravada Buddhism in the twentieth century.
4 Ökotopisches Zentrum in Maria Lanzendorf, Lower Austria, which still exists today.
5 A skirt made from a single width of fabric that is wound around the hips.
6 As a rule, any specialist Buddhist terminology in this book is given in Pali, the Buddhist written language of the Pali Canon. However, for some key Buddhist terms such as Dharma, nirvana, and karma (Pali: Dhamma, nibbana, and kamma), the Sanskrit version has become the established one and is the one that appears in the *Oxford English Dictionary*, and so exception is made for these.
7 Shunryū Suzuki, *Zen Mind, Beginner's Mind*, Weatherhill, New York and Tokyo 1970.
8 Amaravati monastery (in Great Gaddesden, north of London), as well as Cittaviveka monastery, in Chithurst, belong to the Ajahn Chah lineage of the Forest Tradition of Theravada Buddhism.
9 Nyingma, Kagyu, Sakya, and Gelug are the four major traditions of Tibetan Buddhism (Vajrayana); Nyingma is the oldest.
10 The Pali Canon is the collection of teachings of the Buddha in the Theravada School.
11 Words or syllables used in meditation that are recited repeatedly.
12 Nyanatiloka Mahathera, *Buddhistisches Wörterbuch: Kurzgefasstes Handbuch der buddhistischen Lehren und Begriffe in alphabetischer Anordnung*, Beyerlein & Steinschulte, Stammbach 1999.
13 See appendix 5, p.165.
14 The seven awakening factors are listed in 'Finding the Middle Way'; see pp.35–6.

15 A particular ordination for nuns in the Ajahn Chah tradition.
16 *Samyutta Nikaya* 56:31, 'In a rosewood forest', https://suttacentral.net/sn56.31/en/sujato?lang=en&layout=plain&reference=none&notes=asterisk&highlight=false&script=latin (last accessed 11 March 2025).
17 See interview with Ute Hüsken in appendix 4, pp.157–63.
18 Candidate for the siladhara ordination; see appendix 1, p.147.
19 See note 8 above.
20 See appendix 5, p.165.
21 See *Samyutta Nikaya* 56:11, 'Setting in motion the wheel of the Dharma', https://suttacentral.net/sn56.11/en/bodhi?lang=en&reference=none&highlight=false (last accessed 11 March 2025).
22 The word 'guru' literally means 'heavy, weighty'.
23 The principle of emptiness is explained in 'The Power to Say No'; see pp.93–109.
24 The noble eightfold path is explained in 'Finding the Middle Way'; see pp.29–39.
25 'Anagarika' refers to a person who has decided to devote themselves to Buddhist practice and who has given up the majority of their worldly goods and responsibilities. An anagarika or postulant is in a kind of in-between state between a layperson and a nun.
26 The siladhara order is a newly created order for women in the Ajahn Chah lineage, for whom full ordination – that is, bhikkhuni ordination – is still not granted.
27 *Digha Nikaya* 16, 'The great discourse on the Buddha's extinguishment', https://suttacentral.net/dn16/en/sujato?lang=en&layout=plain&reference=none&notes=asterisk&highlight=false&script=latin (last accessed 27 March 2025).

WINDHORSE PUBLICATIONS

Windhorse Publications is a Buddhist charitable company based in the UK. Our books, which are distributed internationally, champion Buddhism, meditation, and mindfulness. They offer fresh interpretations of Buddhist teachings and their application to contemporary life, with subject matter and authors from across the Buddhist tradition, catering for a broad range of interest and experience. In addition to publishing titles exploring classic texts for modern audiences, we aspire to publish books that offer a Buddhist perspective on today's challenges, including social inequality, the environment and climate, gender, mental health, and more. Established in the 1970s to publish the writing of Urgyen Sangharakshita (1925–2018), the founder of the Triratna Buddhist Order, Windhorse Publications continues to be dedicated to preserving and keeping in print his impressive and influential body of work, making it accessible for future generations. As well as high-quality print and e-books, Windhorse Publications produces accompanying audio, podcast, video, and teaching resources.

Windhorse Publications
38 Newmarket Road
Cambridge CB5 8DT
info@windhorsepublications.com

North America
Distributors:
Consortium Book Sales
& Distribution
210 American Drive
Jackson TN 38301
USA
www.cbsd.com/

Australia and New
Zealand Distributors:
Windhorse Books
PO Box 574
Newtown NSW 2042
Australia
windhorse.com.au/books.html

THE TRIRATNA BUDDHIST COMMUNITY

Windhorse Publications is a part of the Triratna Buddhist Community, an international movement with centres in Europe, India, North and South America, and Australasia. At these centres, members of the Triratna Buddhist Order offer classes in meditation and Buddhism. Activities of the Triratna Community also include retreat centres, residential spiritual communities, ethical Right Livelihood businesses, and the Karuna Trust, a UK fundraising charity that supports social welfare projects in the slums and villages of India.

Through these and other activities, Triratna is developing a unique approach to Buddhism, not simply as a philosophy and a set of techniques, but as a creatively directed way of life for all people living in the conditions of the modern world.

If you would like more information about Triratna please visit thebuddhistcentre.com or write to:

London Buddhist Centre
51 Roman Road
London E2 0HU
UK
contact@lbc.org.uk

Aryaloka
14 Heartwood Circle
Newmarket NH 03857
USA
info@aryaloka.org

Sydney Buddhist Centre
24 Enmore Road
Sydney NSW 2042
Australia
info@sydneybuddhistcentre.org.au

www.ingramcontent.com/pod-product-compliance
Lightning Source LLC
Jackson TN
JSHW080335130226
97858JS00005B/19